THE COMPLETE GUIDE TO STOCK MARKET INVESTING FOR TEENS

Learn How to Save and Invest Money in the Market now and Build a Wealthy Dream Future for Tomorrow

Warren Miller

To My Family and

My Little Cookie

TABLE OF CONTENTS

Introduction

We can't even count the number of young adults who have at one time or another watched a TV show about entrepreneurship or read a magazine article claiming that they can be rich too, by investing wisely in stocks.

The idea is appealing to anyone who wants to take control of their future and life decisions, because it suggests that money doesn't matter as much as getting the right investment decisions. Unfortunately, this kind of thinking is dangerous. Not only does it typically take decades for most investors to "get it right"—if they ever do—but there's also no guarantee that your teen will want the same things in 20 years that he or she wants today.

The fact is that for most young people, investing might not be the most important thing in their lives. Until they get older and established in a career, saving and investing for retirement may not be at the top of their priority list; there are other things that might seem more pressing and exciting at this stage in life.

When you're young, you have limited resources to invest. You're also still trying to figure out who you are—what kind of career or education you want to pursue, and how much risk you want to take with your money. For these reasons, it's not a good idea to jump into the stock market before you have a better handle on your financial circumstances and goals.

This doesn't mean you'll never be able to invest in the stock market, but it does mean that you're a long way off from making a decision that will have a major impact on your life. Until then, there are plenty of other ways to get started with investing and the stock market without getting ahead of yourself.

The Basics of Stock Market Investing

To understand how stocks work, you first need to know what stocks actually represent. A company's stock represents a portion of the company's ownership—or equity in it. Think of it as a loan to the company—you are lending them money, and they promise to pay that money back with interest, as well as give you part of the profits from any growth in their business.

If you want to buy stock in a company and receive those potential profits, then you must first purchase shares. For now, it's important to know that stock market investing is simply the process of purchasing shares of stock. Of course, knowing what stocks represent isn't enough— you also need to know how stocks actually work. They can be volatile—and that means that they go up and down in value over time. The simplest way to think about stock market investing is to imagine a roller coaster: the prices climb higher as demand increases. And then, at some point, they drop precipitously; this is called a crash. If you're going to invest in stocks, then you have to be prepared for price fluctuations like these. If you buy at the high of the roller coaster and sell at the low, then it doesn't make sense to call yourself an "investor" because you aren't investing—you're speculating. And this kind of behavior can be extremely dangerous.

CHAPTER 1. Investing: Why?

No matter what your age is, it's important to have a bit of money stashed away. And as you're only getting older, the principle only gains even more importance. Why? Well, because if you don't have any money saved up for retirement yet, or even just enough to get by and not depend on others for financial assistance in case you ever need it in the future then you've got some serious thinking ahead of you. This is why.

To start things off, it's important to understand what investing is and why it's an important topic for everyone you know, whether they're teens or seniors. Investing isn't just about money—it's about planning for your future. Investing is the practice of putting your money into some kind of investment that will eventually pay off some sort of financial benefit in the future. In other words, it's a way to make more money while waiting for the time when you'll need it at a later point in your life. So why is investing important? Well, for one thing, it's the kind of thing that can help you do things in the future if you don't have much money in your pocket right now. Many people start investing because they want to buy a house, buy a car, or pay for their children's university education in the future. Others use it as a way to secure their retirement and avoid becoming dependent on others for financial aid. Whatever the reason may be for you personally, investing is almost always an essential part of planning your financial future. Of course, when you're young, it can be pretty easy to think that investing is only for those who have a lot of money to spare. The point of investing isn't necessarily about the amount of money you've got in your pocket—it's about being smart with your finances and putting some money away for the future when you'll need it.

So if you're worried about having enough money for retirement someday, then starting to invest now can help take care of things for you down the line. But even if you're just looking to save a bit of money while you're still young, investing can still help you out. In fact, one of the greatest things about investing is that it helps protect your money so that it can't be lost so easily. What does this mean? Well, with investing, you have more control over where and how your money is spent. For instance, instead of having to buy something expensive today and then paying for it over time (as in the case of credit cards or loans), your investment lets you pay off the obligation gradually so that you don't have to make such a big investment all at once.

Investing may sound like a daunting prospect, but it doesn't have to be. It's actually very simple and straightforward—you put your money into stocks, bonds, mutual funds or even real estate in order to earn money from the interest or profit these investments generate. The earlier you start investing for your future, the better off you will be as an adult. The sooner you start saving and investing, the less risk there is that one day your egg nest will be significantly smaller than it would have been if you had started saving and investing when you were younger.

If you're wondering how old you have to be to start investing, we've got the answer. First off, it depends on the type of investment: stocks and bonds can both be traded by people 18 and up, while most retirement accounts and IRAs require that you reach a certain age or birthday before you can participate (things like social security). Some savings account also have minimum age requirements—for instance, most savings account for children usually involve parental consent until they reach a certain age. So, when is your birthday? Oh! It's coming up in just one week? Great! In this case, you'll need to wait 12 more months (365 days) before your first withdrawal from retirement fund is allowed. But don't lose hope! You'll be eligible to start investing in stocks, bonds, IRAs and other savings plan once you reach 18 years old.

To help put things into perspective, the average American household headed by someone between 31–35 years old has only $6k saved for retirement. With that in mind, it's clear that many people are having trouble saving enough for retirement on their own—it's been reported that many people end up retiring significantly under the poverty line. That's why it pays to start as early as possible! By starting at a young age, you don't have to worry about being able to save up enough money later on down the line. But not all investment accounts are created equal. Some investments require you to be a certain age to participate, while others may be opened up for anyone to join.

Many parents may be reluctant to teach their kids about finances, but the sooner this responsibility is taken on, the better off your child will be for it. Learning about money and investing early in life will put your child in a better position to start saving for retirement while they are still young. Knowledge of personal finance can help your child become aware of the skills necessary to manage money more efficiently throughout their lifetime and it could help them avoid common missteps among young adults today like living paycheck-to-paycheck or accumulating high levels of debt.

Start Early

When your child is very young, instill in them the importance of saving for the future. Help them to develop a sense of responsibility at an early age by teaching them something as simple as how to open a savings account or start contributing to their college fund. Keep this up as they grow older, and even reinforce the importance of investing when they are just starting off on their own. Children who start young and invest consistently have the best shot at achieving financial security in the long-term.

Tie It into Life Lessons

The best way to get kids interested in personal finance is to make it a priority when you're teaching them other life lessons. For example, if you're struggling with your child to get them to save their allowance, try tying it into a lesson about budgeting. When you allow your children to buy something with their allowance, be sure they know how much money is left in their account. You can even start by explaining how you use budgeting and saving strategies yourself.

Teaching kids about investing when they are young may seem daunting but spending time with them and being an example for them is a great way to help them learn the value of starting early and sticking with it.

Teens are faced with many challenges, and being able to face them head-on is crucial. There isn't a better way to do that than by teaching them about investing.

Investing allows teens to take control of their own finances. Investing can help a teen start making smart decisions early on in life, and hopefully avoid crippling debt later on. Investing also teaches teens about delayed gratification, the ability to work towards and accomplish long-term goals—a skill that will carry over into their future relationships with others as well as themselves. In addition to these more obvious skills, investing can also teach teens about personal responsibility. It allows them to experience failures, set their own goals, and work towards making those goals a reality. By teaching teens about investing early on, they can prepare themselves for challenges that inevitably await them in the future.

Teaching teens about investing is also beneficial because it teaches them to create opportunities for themselves rather than waiting for others to create them for them. A popular example of this is the popularity of "influencers" made famous by Jonah Berger's book Contagious. These are teens and young adults who actively seek out sponsorships from brands in order to create their own income streams. This is huge for two reasons. One, it teaches teens to be proactive about their financial future rather than waiting for opportunities to come to them. Two, it teaches them the importance of strategic marketing—because they have no money being put into their business, they have to find ways to market themselves in a strategic manner that produces results. These are skills that will help teens avoid the debt that so many in their generation seem destined for. By teaching teens about investing early on, they can avoid the pitfalls of debt and instead create opportunities for themselves throughout life.

Achieving Financial Freedom and wealth requires determination, patience, and consistency. More than anything else, you have to be able to delay gratification and stay on the path. You have to be courteous with your resources. If you want Financial Freedom, it is going to take time. It's not something you can buy or happen overnight. Financial Freedom is built over a long time.

Many young people today have not learned how to delay gratification. They expect to have everything they want in life, and they want it now! This is a major reason why they get into debt so easily and live paycheck-to-paycheck. Do you see yourself in this profile? If so, it's time to change your mindset. Stop living on credit and start living within your means. You CAN find ways to save money while you're working hard toward Financial Freedom. You just have to look for them and be willing to make adjustments in your life, especially in the way you spend. People who approach building wealth differently by valuing Financial Freedom know that it requires sacrifice. They have the discipline to put off buying things they want today so that they can buy freedom later on. The key is to learn how to be happy with what you have right now, not focusing on what you don't have or what you can't afford. You have to be more thoughtful, and you have to be willing to accept less in the short-term so that you can have greater abundance in the long run.

If you dig into the wealthiest people's past, you'll find that they were usually not born rich. They had to start from scratch just like everyone else; however, they made a decision at some point that working hard was not enough. They determined that they wanted Financial Freedom and wealth as well, eventually breaking free from the cycle of working for money-paying bills-working for more money-paying more bills—and never getting ahead. This is the classic rat race.

Knowing that they wanted Financial Freedom, these people began to make different choices in their lives. They learned to control their spending, saving and investing on a regular basis. Yes, it was a struggle at first, but after getting through the initial hardship, they created an easier lifestyle for themselves over time. They did whatever it took to get ahead and to achieve their dreams of Financial Freedom. As they became more successful, the more they could live life how they really wanted.

CHAPTER 2. Getting and Managing Money

Step-By-Step Guide to Create a Basic Balance Sheet with Excel

Step 1:

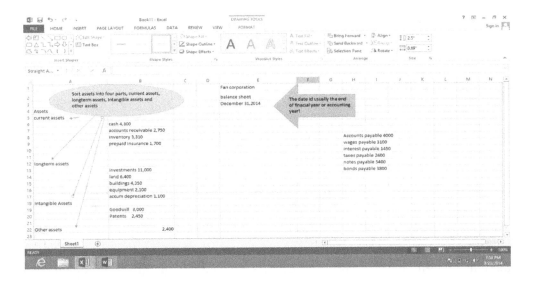

Regardless, compose the title of your financial record. The chief line is the association's name, second line is "asset report" and third line is the finish of the enterprise's accounting time period (as picture shows). From here on out, you need to discover assets and add them into four classes on the left side: current asset, long term asset, intangible asset and other asset.

Finally, figure the total sum of each part and notwithstanding them together to get the total asset number.

Step 2:

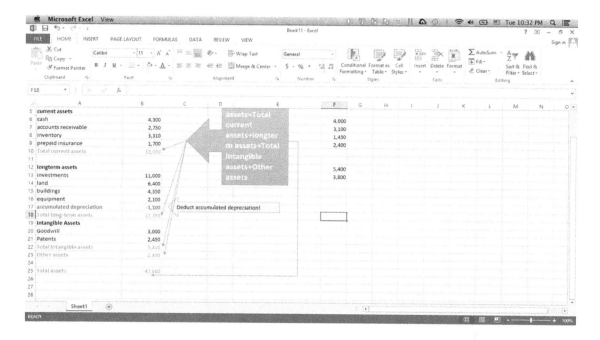

Register each asset class and add them together.

1. Absolute current assets= cash + accounts receivable + Inventory + prepaid security

2. Hard and fast long stretch asset = investments + buildings + gear gathered crumbling

3. Complete unimportant assets = goodwill + licenses

Hard and fast assets = Total current assets + Total long stretch liabilities + Total elusive assets

Step 3:

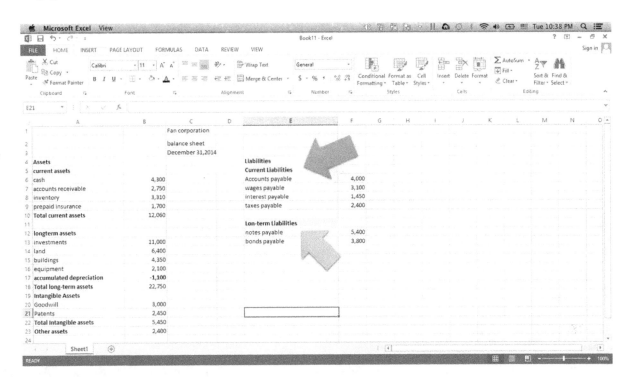

Gap liabilities into current liabilities and long stretch liabilities. Once-over each and every current risk (bank liabilities, compensation payable, premium payable, messages payable) and long stretch liabilities (notes payable, securities payable) autonomously in a segment.

Step 4:

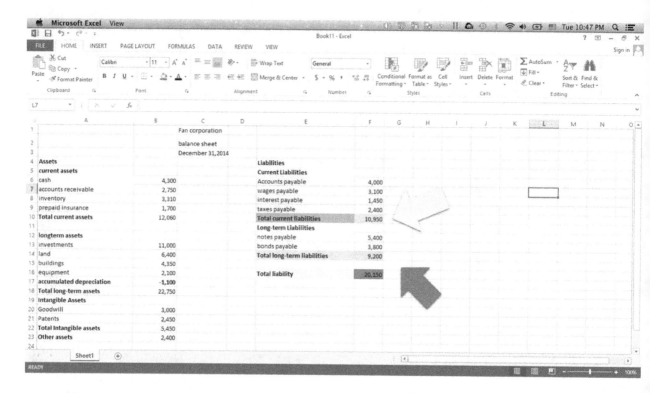

Process the all-out current liabilities and long-haul liabilities and add them together.

1. Total current liabilities = accounts payable + compensation payable + interest payable + charges payable

2. All out long-haul liabilities = notes payable + bonds payable

All out liabilities = Total current liabilities + Total long-haul liabilities

Step 5:

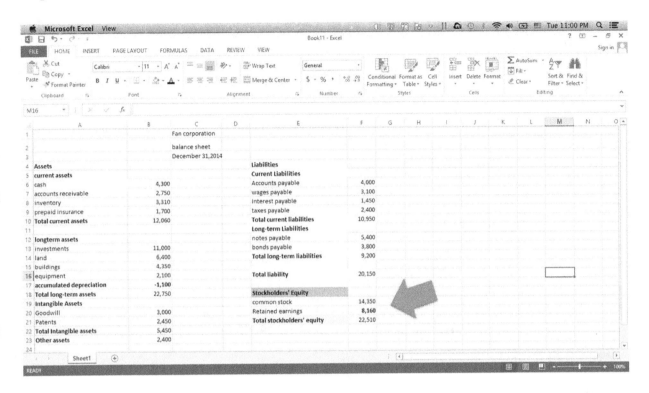

Overview all the stockholders' equity record and process the complete number.

Step 6:

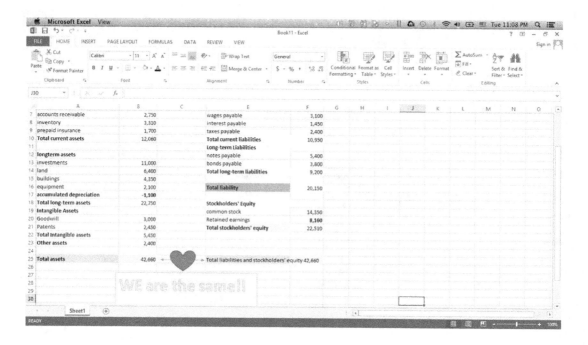

Gather Liabilities and Stockholder's record into a single unit to get the sum comparable to add up to assets.

Warren Miller

Here is a picture of a sample balance sheet of a company:

Balance Sheet
For Year Ending December 31, 2013
(all numbers in $000)

ASSETS		LIABILITIES	
Current Assets		**Current Liabilities**	
Cash	$500	Accounts payable	$650
Accounts receivable	150	Short-term notes	230
(less doubtful accounts)	-188	Current portion of long-term notes	180
Inventory	150	Interest payable	45
Temporary investment	10	Taxes payable	30
Prepaid expenses	5	Accrued payroll	45
Total Current Assets	$627	**Total Current Liabilities**	$1,180
Fixed Assets		**Long-term Liabilities**	
Long-term investments	$400	Mortgage	$960
Land	889	Other long-term liabilities	450
Buildings	506	**Total Long-term Liabilities**	$1,410
(less accumulated depreciation)	-120		
Plant & equipment	447		
(less accumulated depreciation)	-200	**Shareholders' Equity**	
Furniture & fixtures	98	Capital stock	$400
(less accumulated depreciation)	-78	Retained earnings	-421
Total Net Fixed Assets	$1,942	**Total Shareholders' Equity**	($21)
TOTAL ASSETS	$2,569	TOTAL LIABILITIES & EQUITY	$2,569

Setting and Reaching Short-Term Goals (Buy a Videogame) and Long-Term Goals (Buy a PlayStation)

We all want to reach our goals, but it's sometimes difficult to set and stick with them. They feel daunting. But the truth is that small goals are more manageable and help you motivate yourself to continue taking steps forward. I will outline how I've been able to set achievable short-term goals (such as buying a videogame) and long-term goal (such as buying a PlayStation).

Short-Term Goals can be outlined in the form of:

"I will buy a videogame by next Friday" or "I will save $200 dollars by next Thursday." Long-Term Goals can be defined as: "I will buy my own PlayStation by April 2020."

I will do this by:

"I will save $200 by next Thursday."

I am able to set these goals by writing them down on a sheet of paper and crossing them out as I achieve them. This helps me feel accomplished and rewarded. It also helps me realize that I'm actually able to accomplish the goal, since it's in front of me.

If you want to achieve your long-term or short-term goal, you must first realize that it is possible. You must believe in yourself. If you don't believe you can do it, then why would anyone else?

Next, you must set up a game plan. What are the steps that you will take to reach your goal? This is where writing things down comes in handy. When I set a goal, I write my steps, step by step and create an action plan and timeline for reaching them.

Once the game plan is made, it will be easier to stick to it. You should also look for ways to motivate yourself along the way—this can be anything from buying a new book about your goal to going out for ice-cream after hitting your daily step count. It's important to also think about how you're going to reach your goals in the first place. If you want to lose weight, exercise is an obvious solution. If you want to save money, putting more of your income into savings or investments is a good idea. Whatever way you choose to reach your goal, it will help if you put a bit of time into planning how you'll get there. Remember that setting small goals and achieving them will push you toward the larger one. For example, if my goal is to improve my running times by 10 % over the next 6 months. But first I will set a 1000-meter race (220 yards) to run in 90 seconds. Then I will set 905 meters (3 quarters of a mile) to run in 90 seconds. This will eventually lead to running a 3000-meter race (1 mile) in 2 minutes 20 seconds.

The idea here is that I achieve sprints (small goals) on the way to achieving bigger goals. This is a good way to set goals because it gives you a sense of stability and makes you feel confident that you can accomplish your big goal.

How to Earn Your Own Money and Increase Your Goals-Budget

There is a wide range of ways wherein you can bring in your own cash.

The first "way" is called "pocket money." It's the point at which a grown-up gives a kid a specific measure of cash every week, usually between $5-10 AUD (Australian Dollars). Sometimes it tends to be pretty much than this relying upon how much the parent earns and the age of the youngster. The parent gives the youngster the money every week, usually on a Friday or Saturday. The child can spend it anyway they like, however they must be honest. It's sometimes called "remittance." You can also "win" or get money from others like relatives, yet this is less basic than pocket money. On the off chance that you bring in your own cash—and if it's for your own goals—it's easier to contact them because you don't need to ask others for your money. The second "way" is called gifts from relatives (like parents or grandparents). This happens when a grown-up gives a youngster some cash either for a special occasion or just something that occurred in their life (like getting passing marks at school). Gifts from relatives is similar to pocket money, however it's usually given for a special occasion in the youngster's life such as a graduation, birthday or Christmas. The third "way" is known as a summer job. This is the point at which a grown-up gives a young person (usually 14–17 years old) some cash every week as well as some additional things like mid-day breaks and available time. It's known as a "summer job" because it usually happens throughout the summer before secondary school or university. The money is mostly spent on different things, however it tends to be used to arrive at goals.

Where to Put Your Money: Piggy Bank Vs. Money Account

Would you put your money in a piggy bank or deposit it into a bank account? What are the pros and cons of both options? Here we will discuss the benefits and pitfalls of both, so you can decide for yourself. Piggy banks are brightly colored containers that hold coins and cash. These containers come in many shapes, with collectible items like Star Wars characters or Disney princesses on them. The problem with piggy banks is that they're not insured—if they get lost, broken, or stolen there's no refund. In contrast to a free piggy bank account is an actual saving account at a financial institute like TD Canada Trust. These accounts come with a number of benefits, including safety and protection against theft.

The Benefits of Piggy Banks

Piggy banks are ideal for children learning to save, as they are easy to use and allow kids to see their money grow. Piggy banks are also a great way to teach your kids that saving is important and that they can earn interest on their money by keeping it in the bank—even if it's a piggy bank!

The Downside of Piggy Banks

The main problem with piggy banks is that no matter how cute they look, cash and coins left in them will simply sit there, not earning any interest. That's because piggy banks aren't insured or regulated like banks are. This means that there's no free insurance if your bank gets lost or stolen.

The Benefits of a Money Account

A money account is a financial safety net that lets you make deposits and withdrawals at any time. This means that your money is insured by the government if you deposit it in an account at a bank or financial institute (like TD Canada Trust)—so it's protected from theft.

You can also open up savings accounts for your children. This way, you can deposit money into their accounts to teach them about saving while still protecting their money from them. That way, when they want to buy something, they'll be limited to the amount of money in their account, and won't have access to any more cash than that.

The Downside of Money Accounts

Money accounts are great for peace of mind—who wouldn't like to know that their cash is protected? However, savings accounts typically don't earn much interest at all—not enough to make it worth depositing money into them for any real length of time. The interest rates for savings accounts are so low that it's not worth keeping money in a savings account—you'll be better off if you keep your money in your chequing account.

Savings Account Teen-Friendly

A teen-friendly savings account is one that has:

- **Low fees:** It's important not to overpay on fees because the money saved will add up to a significant sum of money. For example, if you bank with Chase and are charged $4 for using a non-Chase ATM, you'll pay $96 in ATM fee charges per year, which would have grown to over $5000 had it been invested conservatively. And don't forget about overdraft protection fees!

- **No monthly minimum:** You shouldn't be penalized for not having much money to save because of having a high minimum balance.

- **Access to ATMs:** In order to avoid fees and keep your balance accessible, choose a bank that has an ATM network or allows you to use other banks' ATMs. And if possible, choose an account that lets you withdraw cash from a teller for free.

Tip: With the exception of the account at First National Bank, all accounts in this table charge monthly fees unless you maintain a sufficient balance to waive them. If possible (depending on how much money is available), pick a savings account with no minimum balance requirement and low or no fees.

CHAPTER 3. Business and Financial Concepts

We will explore what business and financial concepts are, how they make the world of investments work, and what you can do to apply this knowledge in your own life. Business and financial concepts are broad areas of study with a range of subfields. These include accounting, finance, economics, law & ethics, marketing, management & leadership, organizational behavior and sociology.

There is no single definition for "business" or "financial concept," but both can be generally defined as systematic attempts to make money through selling goods or services for profit.

In the broadest sense, a good or service is something that people are willing to pay for. A bus driver obviously needs to make money, but they often get paid for driving (and associated time and energy) rather than by selling a product or service.

A factory worker who is paid an hourly wage will receive minimal money depending on how much work they do, but in many cases won't be expected to sell anything at all.

The concept of "value" comes into play here as well: if workers were only paid based on how much value their efforts produced, then a worker who produced twice the goods as another would potentially earn twice as much pay. As a result, many employers pay employees on an hourly basis which is then divided by the number of hours worked to get an effective hourly rate. This is then adjusted by adding on a fixed amount to get a total take-home wage which may include "extras" like health insurance or retirement benefits. In this example, the worker contributes their time and energy to producing goods or services that are in demand. The employer in turn sells these goods or services for a profit.

As long as both parties see value in the exchange, it will continue to happen.

One important note about market value is that its relative nature means that what is valuable to one person may not be valuable to another. For example, due to higher wages, food service workers in the United States have a greater purchasing power than agricultural workers in India. The agricultural worker will value rice more than the American worker because they have less money to spend and rice fills their daily nutritional requirements.

In a similar way, an investment manager who works 80 hours per week may only be able to afford $20 worth of groceries whereas an idle housewife may easily spend $200 on a shopping spree. This relative value is called "opportunity cost" and it has important implications for investment. We'll discuss opportunity cost more in a future post.

One of the essential things that separates people from animals is the ability to think and make decisions. For instance, if you were starving and someone handed you a slice of pizza, you could eat it. If you were given an entire pizza and told that it was poisoned, you would likely avoid eating it, even though it is literally the same amount of food as before.

This process of analyzing and making decisions based on information that we've gathered is referred to as critical thinking. As you can see, it's an important skill when it comes to business and finance because it helps us make the right decisions about what to invest in and how much money to risk.

In addition, decision-making skills are important for entrepreneurs who must weigh important variables when deciding what kind of business or product to start. For example, if your great idea is a hamburger stand with $5 burgers, that's not going to be a successful business in some parts of the world where people have less money.

At the same time, if you choose to start a $5,000-per-plate restaurant you'd better make sure you're able to get enough customers to earn your investment back and more.

Human communities have been upholding laws for as long as we've been around. Laws are important because they regulate behavior and ensure that people can live and work together in an orderly way. Without these rules we'd have chaos!

Of course this doesn't mean that there aren't situations where rules or laws are broken, but many of them exist for a reason.

Businesses have similar rules: they must abide by the law in every country that they do business in. In addition, they must follow both internal company policies and government regulations. These rules help ensure the long-term viability of organizations by making sure that they don't lose money through illegal or unsafe business practices.

Financial concepts are all around us, influencing our decisions every day. The course of history has been shaped by powerful people making good financial decisions, and ruined by those who made bad ones.

For example, if the Roman emperor Caligula had made better financial choices early in his reign, he might have avoided bankruptcy and a brutal assassination at the hands of rivals jealous of his power. On a more positive note, the financial decisions of the leaders of the United States have helped to create one of the world's largest and most prosperous economies. Financial intelligence involves using our knowledge to make smart decisions and solve problems when they arise. It also gives us tools we can use to plan for all aspects of our lives, both current and future. In particular, financial intelligence helps us make smart investments that will help us reach our long-term goals and dreams.

The Power of Compounding Interest

Compound interest is a form of interest that accumulates and results in earnings on earnings. Compound interest can be thought of as "interest on interest."Let's make a distinction immediately: simple or compound interest? Simple interest is the one defined above, while compound interest is interest on interest.

We contextualize simple interest and compound interest both in the world of financial investments, which is what interests us specifically. Simple interest is the return that is paid to you consistently, based on an initial invested capital, which does not increase because you periodically withdraw the earnings.

I'll give you a concrete example.

Invest a sum of $20,000 in an instrument with which you earn 10% per annum, you will find yourself a sum of $22,000 at the end of the year; subsequently withdraw the $2,000 of profit and repeat the same investment with the initial capital always of $20,000. After 10 years, you will find yourself $40,000, or you will have doubled the initial capital.

Compound interest, on the other hand, is based on the continuous reinvestment of the accumulated earnings, without the withdrawal at the end of the year.

Take the same example again but, after earning $2,000 in the first year, invest the total accumulated capital in the second year, i.e. the sum of $22,000 and not $20,000 as in the first example. The initial invested capital will gradually increase after each year and therefore the annual earnings will increase accordingly.

In this second case, after 10 years you will earn $51,875. In the image below you can see what happens in the two cases of simple interest and compound interest.

Initial Investment	$20.000
Annual interest rate	10,00%
Investment duration (years)	10

Future value with simple interest: 20.000+(20.000*10%)*10 =	$40.000
Future value with compound interest without P.A.C.: VF=20.000*(1+10/1)^10 =	$51.875
Simple net interest	$20.000
Net compound interest without P.A.C.	$31.875

	Int. Simple	nt. Compound without PAC
Total capital	$40.000	$51.875
Interest only	$20.000	$31.875

Do you understand the importance of compound interest and why do you have to use it to earn over time? The principle of compound growth has been around for centuries, but the term "compound interest" was first used by Albert Einstein in 1921. Today we owe much of our economic success to the use of compound liability as a means for banks and pension funds to generate income through investments.

In summary, compounding allows you to earn money with some level of safety on your principal investment and it is not just an abstract mathematical theory—it happens every day.

Compound interest formula: $A=P(1+r)\,n$

Where: P=Principal; r=Annual Rate; n=time period in years.

In the image below we can get a visual idea of how compound interest works.

CHAPTER 4. The Stock Market

Primary and Secondary Market

The Difference Between Primary Stock Markets and Secondary Stock Markets: The primary markets are—as the name suggests—the first buyer-seller interaction, where brokers buy shares from their clients to sell on to another client. It's worth noting that this only applies to publicly traded companies. Secondary markets are where individual investors or non-brokerage firms trade with each other through privately negotiated transactions. Both the primary and secondary markets are for existing stock. When a company sells out for a new product or service, they do so by issuing new shares. When this happens, you'll have a primary market to buy them and if the company is successful, then you'll have a secondary market to sell them on. However, it's worth noting that this doesn't always happen as things can get complicated (even more than they already are). Primary markets are an important part of bringing new capital to firms looking for funding from investors to expand. So if you want to invest in stocks, it's likely that you're going to have to start with the primary markets before venturing into secondary markets.

How It All Works

If you're still confused about how primary and secondary markets work, here's more information. Assuming we're looking at the stock market from an individual point of view, you're going to want to invest in a company. So let's say you've decided to invest in Facebook, which was founded in 2004 by Mark Zuckerberg. Before that happened, Facebook needed funding and they got it from venture capitalists (VCs) like Benchmark Capital and Greylock Partners. Once they had the funding, Facebook was free to expand—but they were still backed by VCs.

As Facebook's popularity grew, secondary markets emerged where people could buy and sell shares in the company. This is how you can invest in stock markets—it's a representation of the underlying value of a company. If Facebook was to sell 100 million shares, they'd have to split them up somehow among investors or they'd lose value. The value translates directly from the company share value—if you wanted to buy 10% of Facebook, then that's how many shares you'd have to purchase (and that would severely hurt your pocket).

Facebook isn't listed on the New York Stock Exchange (NYS-E) yet—it lists on NASDAQ instead. There's a lot of technical information behind this, but the main difference is that NASDAQ is a quasi-private market, which means it isn't run by investors—it's run by the NASDAQ hierarchy. It also has different rules than NYS-E, so if Facebook were to list on NYSE down the line, they'd have to adhere to their rules and regulations.

So you decide you want to get in on the action and buy Facebook shares—what happens next? Do you have a broker who handles your transactions for you? Well most people don't deal directly with brokers—these trades are usually made through mutual funds, which are generally cheaper. Mutual funds are a "collection of stocks" usually managed by a seasoned broker and you can invest in it through them. Mutual funds aren't a bad idea for beginners, but you'll probably eventually move on to individualized stock picking—if you feel confident enough to do so.

So now you've bought your Facebook shares through a mutual fund—what happens next? Do they arrive as physical pieces of paper or do they just get added to your account? Well the latter is true—most transactions are done electronically these days. You'll have to check with your broker to see how they prefer to receive your trade, but it's likely that you'll have to provide them with your bank details and the broker will make a deposit into your account. You can also buy physical shares—these are worth more because there's a limit on how many you can hold, so they sell for a premium.When you decide to sell, the same thing happens in reverse. You contact the mutual fund and let them know how many shares you wish to sell and then they do the rest. Once the transaction has been made, you'll receive the money from the sale in your bank account in a matter of days.

So how do you make money? The first way is through dividends—if you own stocks, then you can likely receive a dividend. If Facebook decided to give its shareholders $0.50 per share, then those who invested $100 would receive $5 (depending on the price of their shares). Some stocks pay more dividends than others, but it's usually on a quarterly basis. The second way to make money is to sell your shares for more than you bought them for. This is called a capital gain. So if you bought $100 worth of Facebook shares in 2010 and sold them in 2012, but they increased by $10, then you made a $10 capital gain—which is nice.

Market's Rules

The rules of the stock market do not apply to these individuals. They apply only to smaller investors like you and me. And even though these rules do not change our probability of success, they do change our expectancy from investing in stocks. In other words, following these rules can increase your chances for profit over time by reducing your risk as an investor.

Below are the most important rules you should understand about investing in stocks:

1) The Stock Market is a zero-sum game. This means that for every winner there must be another loser. It's important to note that the players in this game aren't necessarily human, but rather institutions like banks and brokerages.

2) The Market knows more than you do and anticipates your actions. Don't rely on information from other investors or news channels to make decisions about investing in stocks. Instead, rely on your own analysis of company fundamentals, valuations, and macroeconomic factors to make decisions.

3) The Market is highly efficient. This means that no matter how much analysis you do, it will be difficult to beat the market consistently over time. This efficiency explains why index funds have outperformed many mutual funds over the past 10 years. Therefore, your investing strategy should focus on minimizing risk and understanding when to exit stocks, not trying to beat the market.

4) Stock Prices can go down as well as up. There are always two sides of a coin and that's true with stocks as well. Therefore, don't get too excited about raising a stock price more than 25% from its long-term average or you could get burned (see Cramer's Rule).

5) Be an Accumulator. If you intend to save for retirement or spend the money you've accumulated over time, don't expect your stocks to go up more than 25% a year. This will allow you to average out losses and enjoy consistent gains.

Concepts of Risk and Volatility

Risks are potential losses that may or may not occur, and they are the reason we take steps to lessen our exposure to them. Volatility is the magnitude of price changes in financial markets. Together, these concepts form a powerful combination for investors. So what does this mean? Let's break it down.

Risks: Potential losses that may or may not occur depending on future events.

Volatility: The magnitude of price changes in financial markets often represented by the percentage of change over time or standard deviation from a moving average.

Together—Powerful combo for investors: Risk and volatility together can give investors more information on market behavior which they can use to make better decisions when managing their portfolios.

Since risk and volatility are important components for investors to be aware of, we will take a deeper look at these topics, including what each is and how each can be calculated.

Risk: Risks are potential losses that may or may not occur depending on future events. Risk is a forward-looking concept that can be seen as uncertainty of future price or rate of return.

Volatility: Volatility is the magnitude of price changes in financial markets. Volatility is often represented by the percentage of change over time or standard deviation from a moving average. Currency volatility can also be represented in terms of foreign exchange rates between two currencies.

The time horizon for volatility depends on the financial instrument being analyzed. For example, stock volatility may be calculated by day, month, quarter or year while bond volatility may be calculated by maturity or duration. The time horizon for risk depends on the type of risk being evaluated and must allow enough time to adequately estimate future losses.

Stock Market Indexes

What Is an Index?

An index is a portfolio comprised of many securities that represent a market or an industry sector. The most popularly known indices are the Dow Jones Industrial Average (DJIA), NASDAQ, and S&P 500... but there are many other types of indices.

For example:

- The Russell 2000 is an index of smaller companies in the US,

- The FTSE 250 is a UK index of mid-cap companies, and

- The Hang Seng Index is Hong Kong's stock market index.

Index funds have a few advantages over individual securities. For one, since index funds buy many stocks at once, they can buy more shares at lower costs. Warren Buffet often talks about the power of compound interest—this means that if you invest $100 at 7% for 10 years, you will not just have $107 when you're done but rather $219.8. Index funds allow an investor to lock in market returns over long periods of time for far less money and time than it would take to work with individual stocks and still get a similar result! Indexing is a way to invest in the stock market without paying fees to a professional money manager.

Bull and Bear Market

While stocks values have risen generally since the early 22nd century, we have seen periods of declining stock prices and periods when they were flat. When the value of stocks declines markedly in a comparatively short period of time, it is known as a "bear market."

The term "bear market" was coined by Charles Dow during the Wall Street Crash of 1907. A bear market is often part of an economic recession or depression (although not always), and typically ends with strong price increases once the economy recovers.

A bull market is a market that's doing well. The term comes from the image of crowds of people conniving to purchase stocks, pushing the prices higher and higher. A bear market is a stock market where share prices are falling.

A bull market can be seen in the long-term view as one of four phases in an economic expansionary period or as part of a supercycle; likewise, a bear market can be seen in relation to an economic recession or as part of a correction after a supercycle has ended.

Historically, a bear market coincided with the crash. But, in modern times, stocks recovered quickly from the latter event and went on to make new highs.

CHAPTER 5. Understanding Stocks

Types of Stocks and Their Classification

It is much easier to invest in stocks if you know how different types of stocks are classified.

Not only does this help you understand things simpler, but it also helps you to find the right investments for your portfolio. Here are three major classifications of stocks and how they can be identified:

- **Small-Cap:** The stock market defines small-cap as stocks that have a total market capitalization below $1 billion (around). These companies tend to be on the lower side of the spectrum in terms of complexity and stability, meaning that they're higher risk with lower returns on average for investors looking for these traits in their investment opportunities.

- **Large-Cap**: The stock market defines large-cap as stocks that have a total market capitalization above $10 billion (around). Large-cap stocks tend to be more solid investments with low risk but fairly average returns. They also tend to have a longer history of proven success and a higher level of stability than smaller companies, which means that it's easier for them to maintain their position in the market.

- **Mid-Caps**: Mid-caps are companies with a total market capitalization that's somewhere between small and large-caps. They're relatively stable in terms of growth potential, but they also carry more risk than small-caps (though less risk than large-caps). These companies are successful enough to keep up with the larger companies, but they also still have room to grow and develop.

As you can see, all three of these classifications come with their own set of pros and cons, including risk and opportunity. Small-caps are great if you're looking for a chance to take a big leap in your portfolio's growth because they tend to be the most volatile of the bunch. However, large-caps carry a bit less risk but also offer lower growth potential. Mid-caps are able to maintain stability while still allowing the possibility for very heavy returns, though neither of those is guaranteed.

The third reason is that it helps you make sure that all of your investments fall into line with each other so that they're able to work together smoothly without clashing or becoming ineffective.

How Stocks Can Make Money: Dividends and Capital Appreciation

Dividends are distributions of a company's profits to its shareholders. When you invest in stocks, you're buying shares in publicly traded companies. When the company pays dividends, it decides how much money it wants to distribute—usually, an investor would want as much as possible. Basically, any dividends are one of the ways that stockholders can receive some return on their investment.

Capital appreciation is when the value of your stocks goes up over time—and when this happens, so does your investment! If you buy a stock for $10 and sell it for $15 soon after that (and without touching the money), then you've made a capital profit or gain of 50%. It's like buying a car and re-selling it for more money than you paid—it's your profit.

Together, these two forms of returns, are what investors hope for when they invest in stocks. When you buy stock in a company, you expect to be able to sell later at a higher price (and if it doesn't go up in value—then you're stuck with it).

Dividends can be paid out quarterly or once a year. Capital appreciation is not necessarily predictable—but time plays the biggest factor in increasing price of stocks. As time passes, companies earn more profits from their investments and profits from previous quarters (which increases the amount of money that they can pay to shareholders).

Stock Vs. Bond

Stocks and bonds are two of the most common investments in the finance world. Investors might be surprised to find that there is a lot of overlap, but major differences, between stocks and bonds.

Unlike stocks, bonds are not traded on public exchanges. Rather, they are pieces of paper with a set value and years to maturity assigned by the issuer. Bonds are issued for wide array of purposes (government funding, corporate investment) with many covenants that allow them to be traded on secondary exchanges after an initial issuance date (buying on the secondary market). Bonds also have a much higher interest rate than stocks. A bond is basically an IOU. If you purchase a bond from a government such as the U.S., you are essentially loaning money to the government with the expectation that you will be paid your principal plus interest at some point in the future when the bond matures.

A stock is also an IOU, but in this case it is issued by a private company rather than a government. When you buy stock in Apple (for example), you are essentially lending money to Apple for them to use as they see fit. The expectation is, of course, that Apple will use your money to grow profits and therefore pay you a dividend.

What is the difference?

Stocks are traded on public exchanges such as the New York Stock Exchange (NYSE) or NASDAQ while bonds are traded on secondary markets. There are many exchanges for bonds including the New York Stock Exchange and even bond-specific exchanges. These exchanges can trade globally around-the-clock as opposed to stocks which operate during pre-set hours each day.

Stocks generally have a much higher annual interest rate than bonds which can be as high as dozens of percentage points more than government-issued bonds.

Stocks can be bought and sold on secondary markets with greater ease than bonds which are generally only good for one trade. Bonds are sold at par value and then traded after so you are buying or selling a piece of paper (or electronic representation thereof) with an underlying value and par value.

How Stocks Are Traded

Stock trading is a way for investors to get a percentage of the profits generated by publicly-traded companies. Investors can purchase stocks either from an individual or from a broker.

Investors seeking to invest in stocks are usually hoping for an increase in the stock's price. When large numbers of shares are purchased, keeping prices high and increasing demand, this will lead to increased profits for the corporation that produces these stocks as well as larger dividends for investors. This is why investors often hope that they can win big when buying and selling shares on the stock market. Of course, because volatility is always a concern, there's no guarantee that investment will pay off and portfolios can quickly be depleted if risks aren't properly understood and managed appropriately.

To purchase a stock, an investor has to have money available to pay for these stocks. They must then have a brokerage account with which to purchase the stocks. There are two kinds of brokerages; those that buy and sell stocks directly to investors, and those that trade for investors. The former is called a "full service" brokerage and the latter is called "discount."

Before an individual can cause stocks to be purchased on their behalf, they need to open a brokerage account with one of the many online brokers that are available today. These firms allow investors to conduct basic stock trading from their home computer by using Internet-based trading platforms, which offer tools like real-time market data, news feeds and online research capabilities. Investors who are interested in trading stocks can open a brokerage account with the broker of their choice and then deposit money into their new trading account. They will give the broker instructions as to how many shares they would like to purchase as well as where they want their shares of stock deposited.

Depending on the broker they choose, investors may be able to buy direct stocks and trade them online, have trades executed automatically by the brokerage firm at preset intervals or have trades executed more frequently. Most brokers allow investors to buy or sell stocks up until 4:00

p.m., after which time trades are only allowed if there is an "after-hours" market for the stock in question.

After opening an account and depositing money, investors can start trading stocks. Buy orders are placed with the broker and then filled by the company that issues the stock. Once this occurs, account values will reflect current prices for the stocks. Stock orders can be confirmed online or by phone and trades may be executed immediately or at times later in the day when after-hours markets open. After a trade is completed, investors will be able to access their online brokerage accounts to check their holdings' current value.

To sell stock, investors must sell their shares through the same brokerage firm they use to buy stocks. This can be done online or by phone, generally until 4:00 p.m. the same day. After that time, any trades not completed will carry over to the next trading day. Sell orders are placed and then executed at current market prices depending on the time of day the order goes through.

Some Definitions and Key Concepts Learned So Far

Stocks are one of the most popular forms of investments, representing shares in a company.

Certain stocks are more volatile than others, and it is possible for the stock to go up or down for various reasons.

A stock can also be an investment in a real estate property; here, a share is typically referred to as an interest. It can also refer to shares issued by credit unions.

The stock market is where you go to purchase stocks and bonds; it is also known as the equities market.

Stocks are quite intangible, but it's possible for them to be delivered in physical form; collecting stamps can be made into a hobby, and there is a stamp collecting stock exchange.

Some stocks are traded through the phone or internet, like household stocks at home.

When you own a share in a company, you are entitled to receive dividends from profits that the company claims.

The price of the stock fluctuates throughout time, so when you buy them at a certain point in time, you might earn more money if they increase in price over time. If you sell a stock before it expires, you have to pay tax on your earnings, but if you hold them for more than six months after the purchase date, the tax is usually lower. Companies pay out dividends when they generate profits; this money is then distributed among the shareholders. When a company keeps on failing to make enough money or if it doesn't generate any at all, stocks usually lose value and people who have invested in those stocks will suffer losses.

If you buy a share at 10 dollars and sell it two days later for 20 dollars, your profit would be 10 dollars minus commission costs.

If you have a 200 dollars stock portfolio, you can diversify by buying stocks from several companies.

Companies are established to create profits and the shareholders are therefore entitled to receive part of those profits; this is the reason why dividends exist.

If you own stocks in a company, you are entitled to vote for it on certain matters concerning company policy and shares.

Shareholders elect the board of directors, which is responsible for running different administrative duties at the company; they also approve different financial matters and even have an advisory role in many areas.

CHAPTER 6. Evaluating Stocks

Learn to Evaluate Companies and Their Numbers

A stockholder is a member of the public investing in a corporation for profit. They have a direct interest in the success of the company and its activities. It is therefore essential to use proper guidelines when assessing the value of an individual company. The following information will help you when evaluating companies for potential investment. The income statement provides an indication of how well a business is being run. It gives essential information about sales, costs, profits and assets used in the business at various times over a period of time. The balance sheet shows the financial strength and stability of a company at one point in time such as year-end, rather than with respect to time periods as with income statements. The statement of cash flows gives a picture of the operating cash flow of an organization. It is like a statement of income with an analysis provided for changes in working capital, investments, debt and equity. The gross margin ratio, used for comparing companies in the same industry, shows gross profit as a percentage of sales. The first thing to determine is the fair value of the company. You can gain a lot of information from the annual report, particularly the notes to accounts (if applicable) and also from an investor relations website. It is not a one-step process; you have to take into account various factors. Generally there are two methods which can be used: A discounted cash flow analysis (DCF), which models future cash flows, including growth and capital expenditure requirements against an assumed cost of capital. The discounted future cashflows are then added together to arrive at a value for the business. A DCF model can be used to modify the assumptions to gauge how changes in those assumptions could impact valuation. The variables in a DCF model include: A simple price-to-earnings ratio (P/E), which is one of the most popular methods for valuing a company. It is arrived at by taking the company's earnings per share and dividing it by its current stock price. This method has its limits; there are many factors that influence earnings, which in turn impacts the P/E ratio. An example of this would be an extra expense caused by an unforeseen event, such as litigation costs or a major competitor going under. Good companies tend to have lower

P/Es but the downside is that once the sector matures, competition will mean the price-to-earnings ratio will drop.

Does it have good profit margins?

The higher the better as long as expenses are not out of control and do not account for too high a percentage of total revenue when compared with other companies in the same sector or industry. The ideal profit margin would be in the upper quartile of its sector or industry peers. To find this out, you can consult a company's annual report or from an investor relations website. Does the company have a good return on equity (ROE) and/or return on assets (ROA)? These would also be revealed in the annual reports and reported by an investor relations website. ROE should be equal to or more than that of its peers. ROA should be at least higher than its peers. It is worth noting that these two measures are used as benchmarks by analysts but are not perfect because factors other than efficiency influence them.

Is it earning money?

Gross profit percentage should be high and should be equal to or more than its peers. It is a good measure of how much after-tax profit a company is generating from sales. Gross profit is calculated by removing cost of goods sold from revenue and adding back depreciation and amortization expenses. The percentage can be compared with peers in its sector or industry by going through annual reports or checking an investor relations website. If it has a cash burn or, worse still, is losing money, that's not good. The company should be able to earn at least enough money to pay for its ongoing operations and capital expenditure requirements as well as paying the interest on its loans. It is best if it has some cash left over which could be paid out as dividends or used in other ways such as buying back shares or investing in more profitable activities. If there is a significant difference in the amount of money it earns and the money it uses up, then that either means that there is too much capital expenditure required to maintain its current business activities or it is spending too much on interest payments on loans and other financial instruments.

Essential Stock Measurement

Whether you are a beginner or an experienced trader, there is always room to learn more about the top three stock measurements: market capitalization, outstanding shares, and EPS.

Market capitalization is calculated by multiplying the company's outstanding shares by its share price. Shares outstanding are how many of each company's stocks have been issued to shareholders. And finally, EPS shows the annual earnings per share of a company for the last quarter or year. These stock measurements are used by the financial markets and give you an idea of how a business performs financially. Market capitalization, outstanding shares, and EPS can be used to determine whether or not a company is undervalued or overvalued. You can use these stock measurements for your trading portfolio and research more information about companies that you are interested in trading with. *Market Capitalization*: Market capitalization gives investors a quick idea of the company's size versus other companies in its industry. If there are two companies with similar fundamentals, market capitalization may help you decide which one to buy. The market capitalization of a company is most often used to compare companies or industries.

Shares Outstanding: Shares outstanding are how many shares our company has issued to shareholders. This data can help us decide whether the company is overvalued or undervalued. Suppose we purchase a stock that has a high amount of shares outstanding. In that case, it's usually not because of the earnings per share but rather because the company thinks that there is still some room to grow and issue more shares after they've been floated to shareholders. As an investor, you should keep an eye on our position in companies with an excessive number of outstanding shares when determining whether or not the stock price is overvalued.

EPS: Earning per share is the amount of money the company has made in the past year. If a company made $3 million last year, then had an EPS of $2 per share, you would calculate that the annual earnings per share were $2 million. EPS data can also help determine whether a stock is overvalued or undervalued. If a stock has high EPS and, therefore, good earnings growth, we may think it should be more expensive than it is. On the other hand, if a stock has low EPS and loses money, we may think it's undervalued.

Stock's Split

Stock splits are one way that companies try to make their shares more attractive to investors. When this happens, every shareholder sees the number of shares they own double—but the price stays exactly the same. And while shareholders might seem like they've lost something by not owning twice as much as before, in reality, they now have ownership in twice as many companies.

Warren Miller

CHAPTER 7. Buying and Selling Stocks

Stocks are pieces of ownership in a publicly-traded company. This is a method of raising money when starting a business, without actually giving up control over your company. It's also used for two situations: 1) businesses that have been in existence for several years that need extra cash to expand their operations, and 2) investors who need an investment vehicle for the long-term. The investors have purchased the stock with the expectation that its value will rise when a public corporation decides to sell shares to the public. You can also buy stocks on margin, which means you loan money from your broker to buy more stocks than you can afford to pay for in full at once. Stock trading—also called buying and selling stocks—is the process of buying one or more shares in a publicly-traded company. This gives you a financial stake in the company and entitles your name to either an equity or debt interest. Let's take a look at what it takes to buy stocks today.

How to Buy Stocks?

In order for a company to raise money and/or sell stock, they must publish or obtain a document that details:

a) The type of business the corporation is engaged in.

b) The specific shares available (the class or series).

c) The number of shares being issued, the par value per share, and whether there is a minimum subscription amount.

d) How sales will be handled (e.g., over-the-counter markets, U.S. Securities and Exchange Commission markets), who is authorized to sell the stock, etc...

e) Risk factors of the offer.

f) The company's financial statements.

g) Fees associated with the sale of the stock, such as those for registration services and brokers' commissions, if any.

h) Other important information such as an investment prospectus, pro forma statement, and other supplementary material.

Buying stocks can be a great way to secure your financial future... it can also be incredibly dangerous. So before you jump into stock trading without fully understanding the organization you are buying shares in, it is vital that you know what to look for in a company before buying its stock.

5 Tips for Buying Stocks

1. Have a Plan

2. Research Your Candidates

3. Look Before You Leap

4. Be Prepared to Lose Money

5. Be Ready to Act

How to Sell Stocks?

Selling stocks is the opposite of buying stocks. You are selling your shares to someone else. Just like with buying stocks, there are also many ways to sell them. You could sell them over-the-counter, through a stock exchange, or even over the internet.

Stocks are issued by corporations for raising money and/or publicly trading shares. They can be easily bought and sold just like any other financial security in exchange for legal tender (money). Stocks can represent either equity (ownership) interests in a firm or debt obligations of a firm, known as bonds. The stock market is the main financial market where stocks are traded. The New York Stock Exchange (NYSE), NASDAQ and other large exchanges are institutions designed to buy and sell stocks. There are many smaller stock markets around the world like the London Stock Exchange (LSE) and Japan Securities Dealers Automated Quotations (JPX).

Corporations issue stock in a process known as initial public offering or IPO. In this process, free shares are offered to the public through brokers, who will charge a commission for their services. The issuing company will use the money raised from selling these shares to fund operations or expand its business activities.

Buying and Selling Strategies: *growth* investing and *value* investing and their combination.

Growth Investing

Growth investing is all about choosing stocks that have a lot of potential and buying them while they're still undervalued. Let's illustrate that with an example. Suppose you buy a company with a price-earnings ratio (or PE) of 20 times in 2007, but the market suddenly crashes in 2008. In 2009, the PE ratio will soar to 30 times. At this point, it's time to sell if you want to make big money. On the other hand, suppose you bought a company with a PE ratio of 20 times in 2007, but in 2008 the market crashed, and its PE ratio became 10 times. In this case, you really didn't need to sell it because its PE ratio was still high. It's just that the stock price went down due to market conditions.

So, growth investing is all about buying shares of a company when its stock price is at an all-time low, and then selling shares when the share price is at an all-time high.

Value Investing

What is value investing? In essence, the basic principle behind value investing asserts that a company's stock price doesn't equate to its true worth. If this principle is correct then a company with seemingly mediocre prospects might still be undervalued and thus worth more than its current share price. Value investors seek out such opportunities to profitably purchase stocks at an advantageous price, then turn them around for a profit when the market realizes they are undervalued and prices them higher. Value investing can be broken down into two types of investment strategies, growth and value. Growth investors focus on buying stocks whose stock prices are expected to rise more than the market in general over the long-term due to the company's strong prospects, potential for rapid earnings growth and higher future dividend payments. Value investors focus instead on buying stock at a discount to its real (and sometimes hidden) earnings power (its true intrinsic value).

Combination of Growth and Value Investing

The stock market is the ultimate game of chance but there are ways for savvy investors to stack the odds in their favor. One way is by combining stocks that show promising growth with those generating returns through sound financial management. This strategy has been proven time and again as an effective way for investors to increase their capital while minimizing risk.

Companies that show potential for growth are exciting to watch. They expand into new markets and introduce new products, often expanding their revenue base at a rapid rate. Growth companies typically enjoy higher share prices because investors are enticed by the promise of future earnings. This is why investing in growth stocks is so powerful; if a company increases sales by 20 % a year it could see its revenue rise by more than half each year! This isn't to say that all growth companies will perform well in the long-term; there's always the possibility that they'll be unable to keep up with the pace of their competitors, or simply fail to adapt to changing circumstances. The biggest risk with growth stocks is that potential earnings growth (and revenue) will slow to a crawl or even reverse direction. For this reason, it's important to pair growth stocks with value stocks. Value companies are companies that have generated strong financial results while working within the constraints of their market environment and economic climate. They are able to grow, but in a controlled manner. Before investing, it's important to learn more about how each company's management team handles the tricky task of managing shareholder wealth effectively while still providing investors with a healthy return on investment.

Both growth and value stocks are valued based on their dividend income and earnings per share, but the way a company is valued is determined by the price-to-earnings ratio (P/E). Valuation is measured by dividing the stock's price by its earnings. Companies that are trading below their

P/E ratio are considered undervalued; these companies typically see higher returns in the long-term.

Buying on a Margin

Margin buying is the process of borrowing capital from a broker in order to buy equity securities. This form of trading is only available for those who can afford it, unless the company has an arrangement with their brokerage firm that permits employees or directors who are not "technically" qualified to trade stocks on margin.

Margin buying will often result in both gains and losses on the account where borrowed funds are being used; this may take a toll on your pocketbook if you do not have sufficient cash reserves in comparison with your stock holdings.

The investor borrows the money and pays interest on it to the broker. The investor buys stocks with the borrowed cash. The portfolio is then monitored daily, and an investor will know whether to buy more shares based on what happens in the marketplace.

For example, if you have $10,000 in your account and you want to buy 1,000 shares of XYZ at $5, then you will be buying on margin. Your broker may allow you to borrow an additional $8,000 so that your total purchase price is only $13,000 (or 20% of your investment). This is called buying "on a margin." If XYZ stock moves higher, you will not have to buy more shares of XYZ or pay for the shares that you already own. They would be considered "free" because your initial cash investment is less than the total amount invested in the stock.The greater the percentage that you invest, and the better your broker determines to be able to lend money, the larger your purchase price can be. You can use margin purchasing for most of your portfolio or just a portion of it.

When buying on margin, it is important to know that you are committing yourself to maintain minimum equity (i.e. maintenance margin) in your account at all times. If the equity in your account falls below this minimum, then an automatic "margin call" will be made. A margin call requires you to add more money to the account or sell enough stock to bring the equity up above the maintenance margin requirement within a set period of time. You will need to contact your broker before the margin call is initiated.

Trade What You Know

How many times have you heard the saying, "*It's better to trade what you know*," only to find that it's not necessarily true? If you're trading silver stocks and the market is going in a bearish direction, what good is it to trade what you know when that knowledge is going to create losses? Before you close your account and say that trading isn't for you, consider that many successful traders trade what they know. It's not enough to trade what they do or think. They must also have an understanding of why they are making the trades. For example, let's say you're bullish on a certain stock. There are three reasons why you shouldn't make the trade:

1. You don't know what the catalyst is for the price move.

2. The new information doesn't change anything about your analysis of this company or its stock price.

3. You don't know why other people are trading this company or its related products right now.

If you haven't done any research on this company and you don't have an understanding of its products or related businesses, stay away from the trade. You can't say with any certainty that you know why people are willing to buy the stock right now. If you don't know why people are trading it, it's not a good idea for you to trade it.

Trading what you know could also mean trading what you do, as in the case of a commodities trader who has experience doing business in Africa. One year ago, he made a huge profit on coffee futures at this time of the year.

His question is: What should he do this year? Should he trade the same way that he did last year, or should he trade it differently because he thinks everyone else will be trading the same way that they did last year?

What does "trading what you know" mean in this case? How do you determine if you should trade the coffee futures in the same manner as last year? Or why would you change your trading approach from last year? You could use a technical approach with a moving average and trend line. Some traders will set up the strategy in advance before they enter into trades. Others may use an algorithmic approach, letting their software program run and set stops and targets. Either way, before you begin to trade, you should ask yourself the following questions:

1. What is my goal for trading coffee futures this year? Am I trading to make money or am I trading to learn more about the market?

2. How much money do I want to risk on this trade?

3. How many contracts of coffee futures do I want to buy?

4. What is my risk/reward ratio for this trade and how much am I willing to lose on the trade?

5. Have I picked a support or resistance level that will tell me when to get out of the trade?

6. What is my exit-strategy if the market tries to pull back before it touches the support or resistance level? Do I ride it out or get out immediately?

7. Do I have a stop-loss order in place so that I can get out of the trade if something unexpected happens?

8. Am I trading only one contract, two contracts, or some number of contracts depending on how much money I want to risk on this trade?

9. Have I decided how much profit I want to make on this trade?

10. Do I have a time-frame for the trade?

11. What is my risk-reward ratio for this trade if the market goes against me?

12. What is Plan B if Plan A doesn't work out as planned?

Using these questions as a guideline, you can determine if you should simply trade what you know or if you should change your strategy in some way. When many people think of the term "trade," they might think of a market where goods or services are bought and sold. But trading, in its most general sense, is the act of exchanging one thing for another. And there's no better time to trade than when you're a teenager—when you have fewer responsibilities and more time to explore your interests.

The following list includes some examples of companies that teens can swap their knowledge for some great perks: Apple, Disney, Tesla, Netflix, Amazon, Nike and Adidas. Sony also has indies games like Journey available that require an age range from 13–18 in order to play it.

While some of these are specific examples, the general idea is that companies think of their younger audience when they design and program their products. Some businesses even go so far as to release mobile apps specifically for teens. As a result, companies find themselves in a unique position to engage with a younger audience. With this in mind, teens often take advantage of these opportunities. With the right computer skills and a willingness to learn, they can contribute something valuable to the business themselves—even if they're just helping out on a project or answering the phones for the part-time hours required in their job description. For example, one high school senior built Apple's Siri-inspired virtual assistant software into his mobile phone app. Of course, this list is far from exhaustive. It's also worth mentioning that not all of these companies are easy to get into. Apple and Tesla, for example, offer internships that require an interview and a college degree—but the internship at Apple may be tough for those who are currently in high school. Netflix requires teens to be 18 years old to join their streaming service; for Disney it's at least 12 years old; Nike and Adidas have age restrictions as well; while Sony games tend to be rated only for those 13 and up.

And of course, most of these jobs can lead to career opportunities, where kids can grow with the company, they have been trading their knowledge with. Some teens even find themselves working in the industry they have been a fan of for years.

Apple

There's a reason why so many teens have an iPhone: Apple designs everything with its younger audience in mind. Take the iPod Touch, for example, which is built with games and apps that appeal to younger users. Today, Apple has over 500 employees dedicated to developing products and services that appeal specifically to teens. That translates into innovative products like the earbuds that come included with the iPhone 7—something that might seem silly, but could be very useful to teens who are always on the go.In addition, Apple has an internship program called the "Undergraduate Program" that has as many as 20,000 applications submitted each year. Although it's geared for college students, high schoolers can still apply and have a shot at landing a spot in the program. According to Apple's website, "The Undergraduate Program" is a broad-based training and development program designed to teach college students about Apple and its products. The company hires 10 students from around the world each year. This sounds like a dream job for any teen willing to get involved in the tech industry— especially since applicants will undoubtedly be able to put that experience on their resume once they get out of college.

Disney

Although Disney is known for its family-friendly content, the company has always had a knack for marketing to younger audiences. It also has an internship program with opportunities for teens who have an interest in the entertainment industry. Disney offers a diverse set of internship positions, which can span from animal care to engineering and everything in between. As part of the internship, interns at Disney can expect to have interaction with senior leaders and get a behind-the-scenes look at how their favorite films are put together. However, there are a few requirements that must be met in order to apply: Interns must be at least 17 years old and maintain full-time status during their internship. Interns are also required to attend seminars, offer insight on improving the parks and resorts, and be able to work a flexible schedule.

Tesla

Thanks to companies like Tesla, it's now possible for teens to look at cars as something that can be stylish and fun. Many of Tesla's vehicles have a dashboard touchscreen in the middle of the car. Not only does it control all of the vehicle settings, but it's also integrated with Apple CarPlay—which is another way that teens can interact and use their phones while driving. In addition to all of this, Tesla also has an internship program geared toward students who are pursuing careers in engineering or business.

According to Tesla's website, internships can last up to 10 weeks, and may include dynamic work environments in one of the company's factories, retail stores or service centers. The most important thing to remember about these internships is that they follow all laws and safety standards. No intern will ever be put in a dangerous position during an internship with Tesla.

Netflix

To be a Netflix member, you have to be at least 18 years old, but there are plenty of opportunities for teens looking to get into the entertainment industry. For example, Netflix offers paid summer internship programs that prepare high school students for future careers in content acquisition and production for the streaming video service. These programs offer participants an opportunity to study how Netflix selects shows for its library and go through an immersive process of learning how to write and produce their own shows.

Overall, the goal of these programs is to have the best possible candidates that can take over the company someday. Considering the positions are paid, these internships are ideal for teens who have aspirations of working in Hollywood.

Amazon

Amzon has a variety of internship opportunities, including many that are geared toward teens. Amazon Warehouse is an internship program that gives participants the chance to learn how to work in a warehouse and how Amazon's supply chain works. Another option is the Customer Service Representative Internship, which gives interns the opportunity to get their foot in the door by getting hired as a full-time customer services representative after completing their internship with Amazon.

This position involves working with customers and training new hires on how to take care of customers' questions and concerns. If you think your teen has what it takes, they might want to consider applying for one of these internships.

CHAPTER 8. Index and Mutual Funds

An index fund is a mutual fund that attempts to replicate the performance of some broader securities market index. Index funds are passively managed (i.e., they track their target index rather than selecting individual stocks). Index funds typically charge low fees because they do not require high-paid managers and because they don't trade often.

Mutual funds are investment companies that pool monetary contributions from many people, which enables investments in stocks, bonds and other securities. Today most mutual funds are indexed for tracking the performance of stocks or bonds according to a preselected group of securities, known as an index. Such indices usually include common stocks traded on U.S. and Canadian exchanges.

An index fund is not the same thing as an index. An index is composed of a set of securities, such as the S&P 500, that represent a segment of the market or economy. An index cannot be purchased; rather it exists to serve as a benchmark for investors who want to track how their portfolios are performing against the market or have some other basis for comparison.

A mutual fund that tracks its benchmark closely is said to be "indexed." Other funds in the same family invest in individual stocks and bonds, and these are not indexed. Indexing has proven itself to be more efficient than active management: The average annual return of actively managed U.S.

To buy and sell index funds or mutual funds it necessitates that you have a record with a broker, for example, TD Ameritrade, TD Trade King, E*Trade, Scottrade and so on. Mutual fund investing is best for amateurs who would prefer not to stress over monetary occasions that influence stocks and may lose cash in the event that they got passionate during conditions such as these. Buying into mutual funds are extraordinary for some investors to get going with since, supposing that they don't have the opportunity to do the examination and buy stocks at that point investing in mutual funds can broaden their arrangement of stocks and help them feel greater.

When buying an index fund or a mutual fund there are three unique sorts to look over. The main kind is called an "open-finished" fund which implies that anybody can buy and sell whenever during the day anyway the individuals who buy or sell on the open market won't get as positive of a cost as the individuals who invest straightforwardly from the organization's site. The subsequent sort is known as a "shut finished" fund which implies that they just offer a restricted measure of offers. When these offers have sold, which can require days or even weeks, the fund will presently don't permit anybody to buy into it. The third and most ideal approach to buy an index fund or mutual fund is known as a "no-heap" fund. A no-heap fund is actually what it says, you won't ever pay any charges to invest in this particular mutual fund. The individuals who invest in a no-heap index fund or mutual fund will get the very value that the organization gets for selling shares.

Something vital to acknowledge is that it takes cash to bring in cash. It doesn't bode well to buy an index fund and clutch it for a very long time on the off chance that you won't reinvest any of the increases from your underlying investment into more portions of a similar mutual fund. Thusly, it is a smart thought to invest sufficient cash in an index fund or mutual fund so you can buy extra offers each time you have abundance capital since nobody can anticipate what the stock market will do throughout an extensive stretch of time.

There are various sorts of index funds and mutual funds to invest in. The main sort is called an "Index Fund" which tracks an index, for example, the S&P 500, Dow Jones 30 Industrial Average or the NASDAQ Composite. These funds will hold each and every stock that is in the index which implies that it expands your possessions by spreading your cash across thousands of stocks. This is quite possibly the main elements of a mutual fund on the grounds that since one stock performed ineffectively throughout some undefined time-frame doesn't imply that all other stocks in the index fund will do inadequately also. Along these lines, since you are expanding your possessions by buying thousands of various stocks with only a few hundred dollars you will encounter less instability in your portfolio.

The second sort of mutual fund is known as a "Profit Income Fund." These funds will invest in profit-paying stocks, for example, those which deliver profits to furnish their investors with pay. Normally these funds will have a huge segment of their property in service organizations, land organizations and even some medical care stocks.

The third sort of mutual fund is called a "Functioning Management Fund" which implies that the manager of the fund can make various kinds of investments other than buying the entirety of the stocks in the index. The dynamic management fund can likewise buy securities, unfamiliar monetary forms or even wares inside your portfolio.

The last sort of mutual fund is known as a "Fund of Funds" which implies that it contains various kinds of mutual funds. When investing in a fund of funds you should search for one that has a few distinct sorts of funds so your cash is ensured against horrible showing in one explicit fund or index.

Whenever you have chosen to invest in an index fund or mutual fund then the most straightforward approach to buy offers would be through the organization straightforwardly since they will charge you less expenses. Nonetheless, in the event that you need more cash to make an immediate investment, at that point there is another approach to invest. You can generally begin with a limited quantity of cash and then reinvest the increases from your underlying investment in a similar mutual fund. On the off chance that you are simply beginning in the stock market it is significant that you don't buy an index fund or mutual fund without understanding what it does. Each mutual fund will normally have an outline which clarifies everything about that particular index fund or mutual fund. In the event that there are any inquiries concerning the fund, at that point you ought to circle back to a call to the organization.

CHAPTER 9. Exchange Traded Funds (ETFs)

ETFs (Exchange Traded Funds) are managed monetary instruments and not OTC (like forex) as they are traded on a controlled market, for example, the Italian stock exchange. For what reason do you need to understand what ETFs are and how they work, particularly in the event that you are new to monetary investments?

I accept that ETFs are indeed "another" investment opportunity that until only a couple of years prior were shut to singular investors. ETFs permit the investor to accomplish more prominent self-rule and freedom from the financial framework; more noteworthy mindfulness in the decision of their investments. ETFs are a straightforward monetary instrument, both in their activity and use: therefore they can be utilized by any private investor who needs to invest their reserve funds autonomously. Consider an ETF a fund dressed as an activity ... in what sense? I'll clarify immediately.

An ETF resembles a fund since it reproduces the arrangement of portions of a fund much the same as a mutual fund (the ETF, notwithstanding, is latently managed while the fund is effectively managed). Both the fund and the ETF permit you to differentiate on the market with a single tick since you don't need to physically choose the protections, however with a single tick you buy the instrument and you have a generally broadened investment.

In any case, I envision that there are significant contrasts between mutual funds and ETFs, incorporating fundamentally lower costs in ETFs. You can investigate the subject in the article *"Contrasts among ETFs and funds: discover the amount you can save each year."*

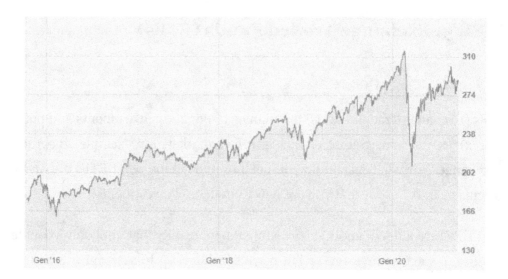

You can consider the ETF as a stock simultaneously on the grounds that you buy and sell it promptly as though it were a stock, at the current market cost. Consequently, from a functional perspective, buying an ETF is totally indistinguishable from buying a stock, yet what changes is the thing that is inside an ETF, that is its huge organization.

To give you a culinary model, the activity is the single kind of a tub of frozen yogurt, the ETF is the tub of frozen yogurt, which can contain numerous flavors inside.

ETFs are an inactively managed apparatus.

ETFs are organized with the point of reproducing the arrival of a reference index (called "benchmark") as precisely as could be expected and not contribution a better yield than the actual benchmark.

This goal is accomplished just by holding the very offers that are essential for the reference index. Buying an ETF, for example, the SPDR S and P500 ETF (Isin code IE00B6YX5C33), is comparable to buying with a solitary snap a bushel indistinguishable from that of the American S&P 500 index, which is comprised of 500 US organizations with the biggest capitalization.

So the presentation of your ETF follows that of the recreated index, accurately the Americans and P500 index.

Mutual funds, then again, are effectively managed monetary instruments genuine manager who pays since it should cause you to get a better yield index.

Sadly in 90% of cases (to be expansive and idealistic) this doesn't occur, yet yo significant expenses each year ... so I encourage you to begin asking yourself event that you have cash invested in funds.

5 Kinds of Exchange Traded Funds

1. - Index ETFs

Index ETFs inactively track a basic index. For instance, the Standard and Poor's 500 Index, which is contained the biggest organizations in the US market by market capitalization recorded on the NYSE or NASDAQ. At the point when you invest in an index ETF, you're investing in a container of protections addressing that specific index. Subsequently, in the event that your investment goes up, at that point this is on the grounds that your fundamental bushel did well too whether it depends on investable indexes, for example, security indexes or non-investable indexes, for example, product indexes.

2. - ETFs that expect to follow a particular index and beat it

These ETFs hold the hidden protections in a similar extent as they show up in the index, however they are intended to outflank it. This implies that if, for instance, you're expecting a huge capital addition in a specific sector at that point you'd need to buy an ETF that intends to follow the benchmark yet with less unpredictability. For instance, you may invest in an ETF that tracks the S&P 500 Index yet invests 75% of its property in stocks with better-than-expected fundamentals, for example, high-income development and low obligation.

3. - Sector funds – US-based indexes

These mean to follow a particular sector, for example, innovation or medical services. In the event that you're hoping to invest in a particular sector, at that point you should consider an ETF that wagers on one of these sectors.

4. - Broadly diversified ETFs

These are like index ETFs and hold a crate of resources and track the index however have a more extensive range of possessions. While this implies more expansion it likewise implies less individual stock exploration is required. An investor who would not like to invest a lot of energy checking his investments may lean toward this kind of fund.

5. - Managed ETFs

These are effectively managed ETFs. They require crafted by an investment manager to supervise their property and are not attached to a specific index.

When would it be advisable for one to buy or sell an ETF?

The overall agreement is that if an individual investor might want to invest in the stock market yet doesn't have any desire to really buy and sell stocks by and large, at that point an ETF item might be the correct investment vehicle. In like manner, in the event that somebody needs openness to wares—yet don't have any desire to really buy and sell actual gold, silver or soybeans—at that point an item ETF will give this kind of openness.

In the event that you are buying a specific ETF as long as possible and intend to keep it there until you need your cash then you can hang on until retirement. Then again, in the event that you intend to trade all the more effectively and have the opportunity to do as such, at that point there might be times when you should buy and sell ETFs.

For instance, if stock markets enter a drawn-out down cycle, an investor may choose to get out there and buy stocks at these lower levels after a rectification to supplant those stocks that are currently failing to meet expectations of their benchmarks. At such a period, selling their ETF offers and buying singular stocks would give this kind of openness. There was one specific person who purchased shares in a little cap esteem ETF against the exhortation of many Wall Street experts. He held his situation during the 2008 market decline and today is quite possibly the most over-utilized, yet additionally perhaps the most beneficial investors out there.

Alternately, if markets are going up for an all-inclusive timeframe as they have been as of late, an ETF investor may choose to get out there and sell their possessions to take benefits. Once more, selling their offers and buying singular stocks would give such openness. As of late we have seen numerous investors who sold their possessions of little cap esteem ETFs to buy huge cap esteem stocks (e.g., iShares Russell 2000 Value Index Fund versus iShares S&P 500 Value Index Fund). While this methodology is an incredible method to support one's wagered, it isn't prudent to roll out such radical improvements at the same time.

While there are a few dangers and intricacies related to investing in ETFs, people who set aside the effort to teach themselves the thing they are buying ought to have the option to maintain a strategic distance from a portion of the entanglements. What is significant is that investors in ETFs recollect that these investments are not resistant to extraordinary descending changes since they may have done above and beyond the long-haul.

CHAPTER 10 Other Types of Investments

Cryptocurrencies

The first ever cryptocurrency, Bitcoin was invented in 2009 by a person or group of people using the name Satoshi Nakamoto.

The idea behind Bitcoin was to produce a currency independent of any central authority, transferable electronically, more or less instantly with very low transaction fees. Since then many other cryptocurrencies have emerged as the value and use of cryptocurrencies has been growing exponentially.

In late 2017 prices skyrocketed for bitcoin and other cryptocurrencies but have since stabilized again. Cryptocurrencies use a technology called blockchain to record transactions. Blockchain is a decentralized and distributed public ledger that is used by cryptocurrencies. It is basically an electronic payment system, in which peer-to-peer users can make payments without using a central bank or single administrator, with the transactions recorded chronologically and publicly.

What number of cryptocurrencies are there? What are they worth?

In excess of 6,700 distinctive cryptocurrencies are exchanged freely, as indicated by CoinMarketCap.com, a market research site. Also, cryptocurrencies keep on multiplying, fundraising through starting coin contributions, or ICOs. The complete value of all cryptocurrencies on Feb. 18, 2021, was more than $1.6 trillion, as indicated by CoinMarketCap, and the absolute value of all bitcoins, the most mainstream advanced money, was fixed at about $969.6billion.

Gold and Silver

In the modern-day and age, our world is one of financial crisis and global economic instability. People worry most about what may happen if an unthinkable event takes place. But regardless, many people are looking for a way to protect their hard-earned money from ever-changing economic trends. Gold and silver investments are one of the best ways to protect your money from lost value in currency fluctuations due in countries with unstable economies. The problem is that many people still don't understand what these investments entail or how they work, which causes them to miss out on a great opportunity to save their hard-earned cash.

Private Equity

Private equity investments are a way to get rich quick. They are short-term, high-risk investments in which investors buy an ownership stake in a company, usually with the aim of reselling it for profit at a later date. Since they're not as regulated as traditional stock markets, private equity deals can offer investors higher returns than stocks and bonds on average. On the other hand, if the market turns against you then you can lose all of your money in private equity investing much faster than you would with stocks or bonds. So although private equity may be more lucrative on average, it's also riskier than other types of investments—and that's something to keep in mind before you invest.

Hedge Funds

Hedge funds are investment vehicles that aim to generate capital gains or income by taking advantage of market price fluctuations. There are many different types of hedge funds, limited only by the imagination and expertise of the fund's creators. For example, a macro hedge fund may bet on currency movements in different countries, while a relative value hedge fund might look for discrepancies in debt instruments with similar risk profiles but different prices. All types rely on sophisticated financial strategies and lucrative information to generate profits. Of course, this is not without risk; all investments come with some kind of chance for loss.

Ethical Investments

Ethical investment is the act of taking your money and investing it in entities that support your values. It's pretty straightforward, really. If you want to invest in a company who isn't going to treat their employees poorly, you can look for companies that have employees with benefits and good working conditions. You can look for companies who don't take advantage of people or resources they shouldn't be using.

The concept has been around since the early 1900s when the idea of separation between church and state came to exist in all that mattered—you couldn't get one without the other if we wanted society to progress as a whole. Nowadays, many people are very supportive of ethical investment and other related practices. For example, one of the ways you can invest ethically is to put your money in banks that support renewable resources and energy sources. If you're looking to invest ethically, the first thing you need to do is remove your money from any banks or institutions that have a bad reputation for exploiting their workers or customers.

#1 – Investments Based on Social Values

Cultural standards direct what is worthy of a specific culture and what isn't. These are normally implanted in various social orders and societies and are generally acknowledged inside that specific culture. Considering the cultural values and what could be gainful to society all in all, preceding making ventures is one type of moral contributing. For instance, a co-usable society is the best illustration of speculations dependent on cultural values. Individuals from a specific culture structure a co-employable and put resources into it. At the point when any individual from the general public requires reserves, the co-usable society progresses cash to that specific part. For this situation, the speculation is made by the individuals from the general public, considering the prosperity of the general public overall—including every one of its individuals.

#2 – Investments dependent on Moral Values

Regularly, this type of contributing would go under the "negative effect" class. A financial backer would not put resources into any industry/company that doesn't line up with his/her virtues. For instance, investors would not be inclined to putting resources into tobacco/alcohol fabricating organizations if the financial backer has solid emotions that such enterprises are against their ethics.

#3 – Investments dependent on Religious Values

Each religion has its own practices, convictions, and culture. What is adequate to one society may not be worthy to another. Individuals from a specific religion/culture would be more disposed to put resources into businesses/organizations that are valuable to their way of life/religion or assembling items that are adequate to their way of life/religion.

For instance, investors in the Middle East would be more disposed to put resources into Hijab/Abaya producing organizations as there is a gigantic interest for it, and it is worthy to that specific culture.

Financial backers having a place with the Judaism confidence would be more disposed to put resources into organizations that cling to their standards—like Kosher nourishments.

#4 – Investments dependent on Political Values

The political environment influences the manner in which the financial backers see the condition of the economy and normally impacts their contributing examples.

Financial backers will in general contribute more and accept the danger to be lower when their ideological group is in force. Financial backers are bound to hold stocks and put resources into long-haul protections during such period. On the other hand, financial backers would be more averse to contribute when an alternate ideological group is in force.

They would be bound to put resources into momentary stocks and exchange all the more frequently. For instance, a leftist would probably put more in the stock market when the Democrat Party is in force and would put resources into ventures that favor the specific party's value framework.

#5 – Investments dependent on Environmental Values/Green Investing

Given the present status of the planet, green putting is quickly acquiring significance lately. Under this sort of contributing, speculations are made in organizations that produce harmless to the ecosystem items, or their assembling measures are economy amicable. There have been numerous examples in the course of recent many years wherein huge scope enterprises have caused significant air/water contaminations. These influence the condition of the climate significantly.

Green putting centers around putting resources into organizations which don't hurt the climate through their creation measures just as the eventual outcome is climate agreeable. It isn't adequate that the cycles are climate amicable if the eventual outcome ends up being something unsafe, for example, single-use plastics or choose renewable energy sources for your home.

Green contributing additionally centers around different organizations which have an ecological agreeable target, for example:

- Protection of existing characteristic assets;

- Finding and delivering elective fuel sources;

- Reusing;

- Tidying up of water bodies;

- Green transportation;

- Decreasing of wastage.

Coins, Stamps and Art

Coins

Some people might think investing in coins is too risky, but there are actually a lot of ways to ensure that you don't lose money. The first thing you need to do is find out what kind of coin you want to invest in. Should it be a smaller coin that has potential for big gains? A more established coin with a lower risk factor? Or something else entirely? Choosing the right investment can make or break your decision so make sure you take the time to understand the different options available for your portfolio. The second step would be determining where and how much money you want to invest. No matter how much you hold, it is still a good idea to spread your money across multiple different coins. Not only does this provide a safety net in case one investment goes wrong, but it can also help with the tax implications as well. Different states have varying laws regarding cryptocurrency so make sure you keep up with the latest news if you are going to be investing from an outside location.

The third step would be to actually make your move and invest in a coin. The ideal time to buy would be during big dips in the coin's prices such as when Bitcoin went from $30,000 to $6000 dollars or when Ethereum went from $1000 to $200 this year. The best thing about cryptocurrency is that there is virtually no way for the market to be controlled by a single party. This is one of the reasons why it has experienced such success in recent years. All it takes is one bad round of news or a regulatory decision to cause coins prices to drop, so if you're in it for the long-haul then now would be the time to buy.

Stamps

A true stamps investor knows both the past and present of this commodity, as well as how to find the best stamps for investment.

How valuable do you think it would be to have a physical commodity that has been used since ancient times for communication? It turns out that these postage stamps were first used in Great Britain in 1840 and the United States around 1850. Hence, postage stamps are not only an invaluable part of the history of communications but also a tangible investment.

Art

The art world has always been shrouded in mystery. It takes a deep knowledge or a refined eye to identify the value of an artwork. Yet, every day, people are buying art as an investment for their future retirement funds. According to the Claymore Group's "2017 Global Fine Art Market Report," more than half of total sales of top-tier art (works valued at $1 million or more) took place at auctions on record-breaking days for most impressive bids. In 2017, Asia was the biggest market for high-end art sales, with collectors from Hong Kong and mainland China leading the way. Furthermore, art has outperformed all other categories of collectible asset over the last 20 years.

The Top Ten Art markets are as follows:

1. China, $8 billion (grew by 20% in 2014)

2. United States, $5.2 billion (up 20% in 2014)

3. United Kingdom, $3.5 billion (up 20% in 2014)

4. France, $2.8 billion (up 15% in 2014)

5. Japan, $1.9 billion (down 1% in 2014)

6. Germany, $1.7 billion (down 3% in 2014)

7. India, $1 million or more per piece (growing 40%)

8. Switzerland, art valued at over $250 million for the first time ever during the period

9. South Korea: art valued at over $250 million for the first time ever during the period

10. Russia, art valued at over $250 million for the first time ever during the period

A sample of works which set record prices at auction:

1. "Nu Couché" by Amedeo Modigliani (1917), sold for $170.4 million on November 12, 2015 in New York City.

2. "White Center" (1952) by Mark Rothko sold for $66.8 million on May 8, 2016 in New York City to an unknown buyer but was later revealed to be Kenneth C. Griffin, founder and chief executive of Citadel Investment Group and CEO of Citadel LLC.

3. "The Card Players" (1891) by Paul Cézanne sold for $250 million on November 11, 2014 in New York City.

In late 2013, billionaire Ken Griffin bought an artwork by abstract artist Mark Rothko for $80.1 million and a Jackson Pollock painting (1948) for $200 million. Bloomberg News reported that he and his wife Anne Dias Griffin purchased the two artworks from David Geffen, co-founder of DreamWorks SKG. *"I collect art today not just because I can afford to do so, but also because I can afford not to do so,"* Griffin said in a press release at the time.

Comics Market (Rare Editions, First Editions, Special Editions)

X-Men No. 1 (Rare Edition)

In 2012, the introduction issue of X-Men from 1963 sold for $492,937 at sell-off. The close mint duplicate acquired a 9.8 out of 10 on the CGC scale, the measurement utilized by authorities to decide the nature of vintage funnies. The issue presented Cyclops, Beast, and Magneto (Wolverine wouldn't appear for one more decade).

Tales of Suspense No. 39 (Rare Edition)

Iron Man was viewed as a B-list Marvel superhuman for quite a long time—until 2008, when the film variation pushed the character into the spotlight. The buzz around Iron Man made his introduction issue from 1963, Tales of Suspense No. 39, a standout amongst other selling funnies from the time when it sold for $375,000 in 2012.

"Stunning Fantasy #15," in which Spider-Man first shows up, slipped to second-most noteworthy Marvel comic at any point unloaded, having sold for $1.1 million of every 2011. (First Edition)

Assassin's Creed Origins TPB (2020 Titan Comics) Special Edition

Composed by Anne Toole and Anthony Del Col. Workmanship by PJ Kaiowa. Cover by Toni Infante. Back Cover by Sanya Anwar and Special Edition of direct connection to the top-rated videogame, *Assassin's Creed Origins* including at no other time seen restrictive substance.

Old Egypt, a place that is known for greatness and interest, is vanishing in a merciless battle for power. Disclose dim mysteries and failed to remember legends as we excursion to the actual beginnings of the Assassin Brotherhood and past!

Superman (1938 - Action Comics #1) Rare Edition

The issue of Action Comics #1, which sold for 10 cents when it was released in 1938, is the world's most valuable comic book. The comic includes the story of Superman's origins and is considered to be the start of the superhero genre, has sold for a record $3.25 million. It is thought only around 100 copies of the comic still exist.

This particular copy was "buried in a stack of old 1930s movie magazines", was in mint condition, and shows the first ever appearance of Superman.

CHAPTER 11 The Right Time and the Right Way to Invest

There has never been a more important time to invest your money in stocks than right now. With the American economy looking good and inflation rates low, you should be taking advantage of this opportunity as soon as possible. Owning stocks can help you make a lot of money with little risk of failure, so let's go over everything you need to do before investing in them.

It's a safe bet that you've heard of the stock market. Many people invest in stocks, bonds, commodities, and other options to try and build up their retirement funds. But when is the right time to invest?

The answer is different for everyone. Some people are comfortable investing in volatile markets while others prefer the stability of government bonds or gold bullion. Ultimately it comes down to your risk tolerance and what you hope to get out of your investment decisions.

Uncertainty is never a good thing, but it does have the positive effect of creating opportunities for those who are willing to take a chance and invest. In fact, it's the most successful investors that take advantage of these situations. If you can't play the game, you can't win! You have to be flexible and ready to adjust your strategy to any unexpected events that might occur. Keep this in mind when deciding how much time you plan on investing in your stocks or bonds.

In certain situations, there are rules that apply to all investors. When deciding to invest in stocks, start looking at companies with steady earnings growth, low debt levels and a solid quarterly report. It's important to keep an eye on these things before investing in them.

You always want to know what your return rate is, which is based on the compounded annual growth of a stock. For example, if you invest in a stock and it has a return rate of 10% then at the end of one year, you'll have made 10%. Multiply that by 4 and you'll see that after 4 years your earnings will be 40%. You will have doubled your investment in only four years.

This type of investment is known as long-term and should be considered by investors who are comfortable with risk. This is because there are no guarantees that the company will continue to have solid earnings and a positive report. If this happens, though, you'll be able to sell your stock and make a profit.

Then there's the option of short-term. This involves taking larger amounts of money in smaller investments because of the faster returns. Basically you are playing the market by buying stocks that show high volatility and fast growth rates, holding them for one year or less then selling them off. This is an option for investors who want to make a lot of money quickly but aren't willing to risk losing it all if they invest in the wrong stock.

The last option is known as fix dividend income investing. You invest in these types of stocks by getting dividends, which are basically a percentage of the company's earnings.

The return rate for this type of investment is rather small and is more suited to investors who want to keep their money safe. This isn't exactly the type of investment your retirement needs but it's good to have something like it as a safety net.

Setting Your SMART Financial Goals

Setting your SMART financial goals may seem daunting, especially if you have no idea where to start. Let's break it down into a few simple steps to make this process less overwhelming:

- Choose a goal as specific as possible for your savings and investments: For example, do you want to save $1,000 or $10,000? Choose the amount that is appropriate for your needs and budget.

- Establish specific dates for these goals by asking yourself what you need them by: Perhaps you need an emergency fund by next year. Or maybe you want to create a college fund for five years from now. Time frames will differ based on individual saving needs.

- Assign a specific amount of money to each goal: After you know how much you want to save for each goal, just break it down into monthly amounts.

- Set up a Smart financial goals system: Once you have established your goals, it's time to put a plan in place so that you can allocate funds appropriately. You can start by setting up an automatic withdrawal from your checking account or a recurring transfer from your savings account into your investment account.

5 Pitfalls to Avoid

1) **Avoid Scams** —This is the one tip that should be repeated 10 times over. As tempting as it may be to make quick money, be wary of any money you can make quickly. The easiest way to spot a scam is if there is an element of secrecy. If someone wants you to give them your credit card number in order to cash out your investment earnings or if they are trying to keep the investment a secret, just run the other way!

2) **Avoid Tax Evasion** —No matter how large the amount that you invest into a product, never buy into anything that does not have your capital gains in mind. Your interest is always in getting your money back with a reasonable profit, and this should always be on the top of your mind when investing.

3) **Avoid Cash Out** —When you invest, you are always hoping to make more than what you put in. Otherwise what's the point? However, when it comes to certain investments that do not have a set pay-out system, never cash out early. The only reason to cash out early would be if you need the money for some emergency, and even then, you should try and use other methods. For example, selling your home or getting a USAA auto loan.

   Even those 40 % returns can quickly turn into 0 % when you cash out early

4) **Avoid ACH Payments** —This one is included in almost every list on avoiding risky investments. While this kind of sounds like a loophole to get away from paying taxes, the IRS has closed it with a cap on interest rates. If you are looking to avoid paying capital gains taxes, do not use an ACH payment system for your investment.

5) **Not knowing your own level of risk tolerance** — Investors often fail to know what their own risk tolerance is when investing in the market. People who invest in stocks should have a "stomach" for risk. They should be ready to endure short-term losses in

order to achieve long-term gains. Knowing your risk tolerance also means that you know the amount of risk you can take. If you have a low tolerance for risk, take on smaller amounts of stocks and mutual funds if possible. You don't want to put yourself at the point where your money is never safe from losing value.

CHAPTER 12 How to Manage Your Investment Portfolio

You can't depend on karma. To win large in the stock market, you must have a strategy. You should utilize rationale and do broad examination. The following are the most impressive portfolio management techniques that you can use to develop your cash and make the best out of your investment portfolio.

Strategy 1.

Try Not to Use Your Emotions in Making Investment Decisions

Charlie is a prepared stock market investor and has brought in a great deal of cash in the past from his investments in the assembling business. Following years and years of winning in the stock market, he chose to invest in games stocks. He examined various games stocks including Madison Square Garden Co. (MSG). MSG claims five pro athletics groups, including the New York Knicks. Its stock worth is somewhat unpredictable and changes habitually, so it's not incredible for long-haul investment. However, Charlie is a New York Knicks fan, so he invested in MSG and in the long run lost a ton of his well-deserved cash.

You will lose a ton of investment openings in the event that you let your feelings cloud your judgment. You should be very target when you're choosing which stocks to invest in. You should save your own inclinations and take a gander at the numbers.

You can uphold your games group all you need, however don't buy a group's unsteady stock since you're a lifelong fan.

Strategy 2.

Diversification

The insightful men of Wall Street always say "don't tie up your resources in one place." Why? All things considered, in the event that you lose that crate, you'll wind up losing all your eggs.

You should share your riches. For instance, on the off chance that you have an investment financial plan of $20,000 don't spend everything on FB stocks. Buy various stocks and different protections. You can invest shortly in stocks and a tad in bonds and testaments of store. One of the least expensive and most straightforward ways to expand your investment is to invest in a mutual fund. You can likewise invest in exchange-traded fund or ETFs and land investment trusts or REITs.

It's additionally savvy to invest a smidgen of your cash in index funds. The best index funds like S&P 500 permits you to claim a tad of the most elevated performing stocks.

You ought to likewise continue to assemble your portfolio. Utilize your investment benefits to expand your portfolio and buy more protections.

Strategy 3.

Stop Losses

Lara claims 100 Company Y stocks that she purchased at $600/share. Following a couple of months, the stock value rose to $800. This procured Lara a benefit of $2,000 ($8000 - $6000).

Lara felt that she could as of now unwind, so she went on a fourteen-day Caribbean voyage. She didn't check her record while still on a vacation. At the point when she returned from her get-away, she discovered that Company Y's stock value dropped to $400. She winds up losing a sum of $2,000.

To hold this back from happening to you, you should submit a breaking point or stop request with your broker to monitor your misfortunes. You can even put in a following stop request so you could determine the measure of misfortune you can endure.

You can stop your misfortunes physically on the off chance that you would prefer not to put in a stop request.

To do this, you need to screen the cost of your investments consistently. At the point when the cost of the stock starts to go down, put in a sell market request with your broker.

To win reliably in the stock exchanging, you need to keep your misfortunes as low as could be expected.

Strategy 4.

Invest in a Company That Pays Dividends

Many "stock exchanging for novices" books will advise you to pick an organization that delivers profits. And that is solid counsel. As a general rule, profit installment means that an organization is doing extraordinary monetarily. Besides, it's a decent wellspring of normal pay, as well. Who would not like to get checks via the post office each quarter?

However, you should recollect that the organization can stop profit installments anytime. Organizations that deliver profits normally have a sluggish development rate since they are not reinvesting their benefits for extension.

Strategy 5.

Non-Correlated Assets

In the event that you need to turn into an effective investor, you don't just need to enhance your resources. It's additionally shrewd to invest in non-connected resources.

How about we take a gander at Tony's and Noel's story to show this point. They are both new investors and they chose to differentiate their portfolio and invest in various stocks.

Tony invested his cash in various informal communication organizations. Noel, then again, chose to take diversification to the following level. He invested in non-associated organizations. He invested a tad of his cash in tech organizations. Be that as it may, he likewise invested a tad in mining, food industry, and oil industry. Following a couple of years, the informal communication industry eased back down and Tony wound up losing the vast majority of his cash. Noel additionally invested in long-range informal communication organizations; however he's actually doing extraordinary on the grounds that his investments are spread out across various businesses. The technique for diversification is presumably quite possibly the main viewpoints in an investment plan. Diversification will assist you with receiving the rewards of investing in various territories and decline your danger. You need to pick investments that will perform diversely during various market conditions. For instance, on the off chance that you are anticipating expansion, at that point stocks that produce more pay will be advantageous during an inflationary period. On the off chance that you're anticipating resigning in 10 years, at that point development investments would be better right now. On the off chance that you just have one kind of investment in your portfolio, (for example, all securities or all stocks), at that point it could seriously hurt your exhibition if there is a decline in that market. In the event that there was a financial slump and loan costs fell, being too intensely invested in bonds could mess genuine up for your portfolio.

Diversify your Portfolio to Minimize Risk and Maximize Gains

Diversification is key in managing an investment portfolio. Diverse investments spread out the risk and help protect against loss. A diverse mix of investments also helps maximize returns, since different asset classes tend to move independently of each other.

In the following chart we see how an investor's holdings are typically divided.

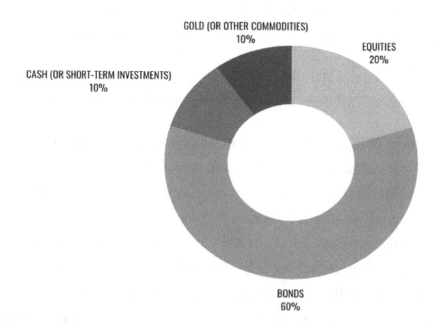

About 20% equities, 60% bonds, and 10% cash equivalents (either cash or a short-term fixed income investment). The remaining 10% should be in a mix of real estate or alternative investments such as gold or timber futures. Each category has different risks associated with it. Below we will talk about the types of risk.

Security Risk

If you are the owner of a diversified portfolio, one way to reduce your security risk is to hold a broad mix of securities. This is because even if one sector in the market declines drastically, the other sectors may be performing well and thus generating income for you.

Exchange Rate Risk

If you invest your money outside of Canada, there is always exchange rate risk. That risk is that the value of your foreign holdings will drop because of the relative strength of the Canadian dollar compared to foreign currencies. In a diversified portfolio, some will benefit and some will suffer from this exchange rate risk.

Inflation Risk

Inflation is always a concern as prices rise over time. A diversified portfolio can help prevent inflation from eroding your income and capital, since different asset classes react differently to inflation. For example, equities tend to do well during periods when inflation rises. Bonds and cash holdings tend to lose value during periods of inflation.

Competition Risk

In order to increase market share and profits, employers often replace employees with newer technology or computers. Traditional investments such as bonds and cash equivalents may not always be able to compete with new technology for people's investment dollars. That means your money is at risk of being diverted into other types of investments.

Other Risks

Any type of investment can have unique risks associated with it. As time goes on, we face more and more challenges in trying to maintain a healthy financial portfolio. In order to do so, it's important that your investments include stocks from different sectors. This way, you're not betting everything on just one industry or company—and you can take advantage of opportunities outside of the U.S., which means more opportunity for growth!

The next time you want to make an investment, diversify! You'll be glad you did when the economy takes a downturn.

Having an appropriate portfolio management can assist you with remaining cold and increment your opportunity to make more benefit from investments with less danger than not doing anything by any stretch of the imagination. I will present a few methodologies for investors who are searching for ways to improve their portfolio management abilities and conquer passionate exchanging issue.

As everybody knows, not being passionate is vital in dealing with your investment. The market is always showing signs of change and sometimes it can go up or drop down in a brief timeframe. On the off chance that you are caught by dread, covetousness or frenzy, at that point you get no opportunity to make more benefit except for rather you will lose cash in spite of the fact that you have wise investments.

Thusly we ought to figure out how to control our feelings prior to exchanging for any investment. In any case it is difficult to make benefit regardless of whether we have great information about investment and exchanging strategies. Few individuals realize that traders can manage the feelings during investing measure by utilizing an appropriate technique called "investing brain science." Also, there are a few techniques which can be utilized to defeat the enthusiastic exchanging issue.

As per Stock Charts, they referenced four stages for you. The first is to define your monetary goals and consider how much cash you might want to place into the investments. From that point forward, think about your capacity to bear hazard and figure out what sort of investment would be proper for you dependent on your danger resistance level. (Bear and buyer market may cause higher unpredictability in investment, yet it doesn't imply that high instability implies higher danger). Thirdly, choose how long you need to keep the investments and figure out what you would do if the market were to decay throughout a more drawn-out timeframe from your buy date. And finally, set up your investment hazard openness in rate terms, which will expect you to consider your age and target retirement date.

CHAPTER 13 Personal Advisor and Online Brokers

The internet has made many things easier, including the process of starting a personal budget. There are many resources available for advice on how to balance your income with your expenses. Personal advisers and online brokers offer different ways to stay on top of every dollar you spend, which is equally important for the personal investor and those looking to buy or sell real estate.

With so many websites out there, it might be hard to know where to start or what information you need in order to get started. We've compiled a list of some of the best sites that will allow you find your way from an initial budget plan, all the way up through retirement planning. By the end of this article, you should have a good idea of what your retirement budget should look like.

A great place to start is by setting a budget. While the initial step in creating a personal budget is deciding where every dollar goes, this isn't the only step in creating a plan that will help you reach your goals. Once you have figured out how much goes to every expense, it's time to create areas for savings and investment. Use this site to get started on plotting out your budget. Then use our recommended broker site as well as other websites for more detailed advice on how to invest wisely and create a comfortable retirement. As a professional investor and general financial advisor, Suze Orman has helped thousands of people plan for their future with strategies for investing, saving, and avoiding debt. Her website provides an easy way for you to start running your own numbers to see how much money you will need to achieve your goals.

After determining how much goes to savings, where should that money go? Most people's first thought is to a savings account. Unfortunately, today's savings account can't provide the returns you need in order to reach your goals. If you're saving for retirement or college tuition, it's important that the funds are placed in an investment that grows at optimal rates. In order to do that, you need to invest in the stock market.

Robinhood is an investing app and brokerage that allows you to invest for free. It also provides all of the tools you could want in order to learn how to invest. This includes getting started guides on stock trading, research tools, educational resources, and even a financial news feed. They'll give you all of the information handouts you need to make informed decisions.

Once you've reviewed their app or signed up on their website, Robinhood will link up with your bank account for easy money transfers. Once the money is available, it's time to get started and start buying stocks. Once you have a portfolio started, it's time to make sure it's growing fast enough. Once you've been invested in the stock market for a certain period of time, it is important to look at your portfolio and see how much your stocks have grown. If they didn't perform as well as you hoped, what should you do? You have two main options. The first option is to sell your stocks and get a return on the current value of the stock. This may result in a small profit or loss, however. The second option is to re-balance your portfolio. This means that you take your current portfolio, and sell off the stocks that are doing worst. Then you move the money to the stocks that have done better, in order to bring everything back up to an even keel.

If your strategy is working well and your portfolio is growing, it's time to make some changes. The first thing you should do is look at how much risk you are taking with your investments. The riskier the investment, the higher potential there is for growth. However, these investments also hold much more risk of failure or loss. For example, the stock market as a whole is risky and could potentially crash.

What are personal advisers? Personal advisers are people who help answer your questions about investing, retirement planning, and other topics so that you can take control of your future. Fine-tuning these decisions may be as simple as choosing the right online brokerage or reading a few articles. That's where an online broker comes in handy. The best personal advisers and online brokers don't just answer questions, but also help you to develop an investment strategy that's compatible with your risk tolerance and financial goals. For example, if you have a few million dollars sitting in an account, you may require a different investing strategy than someone with $50k. In this post, I will show exactly how to identify the best personal advisers and online brokers for your needs.

The first step is to figure out why you need a personal adviser or online broker in the first place. This is an important step because you can't always just compare the prices and terms of different personal advisers and online brokers for a certain service. For example, if you are looking to invest in cryptocurrencies, you will need a very different type of personal adviser or online broker than if you are thinking about buying stocks.

If you're looking for some great personal advice, check out a few online brokers and see what they offer. This can be a good way to compare rates, services, and policies before you sign on the dotted line. You can look at the benefits each of these companies offers before choosing which one is right for you. Online brokers are becoming more and more popular because it saves time and money—no need to drive around to different banks or wait in line! And just because it's convenient doesn't mean that it sacrifices quality or service—many online brokers offer free financial consultations with professional advisors who will gladly help you navigate life insurance options and investment strategies with ease. Once you have your account set up with an online broker, it's time to start looking into what kind of plan you need. Some of the options that you should consider include:

Term Life Insurance—This is actually one of the cheapest forms of life insurance that you can purchase, since it only covers for a certain amount of time (usually 20 years). The great thing about this policy is that it will never become outdated like permanent policies do, so even if you don't need protection after the first twenty years, the policy will still be good in case you need coverage at a later date.

Universal Life—This type of insurance plan provides multiple options for death benefits along with flexible premium payment plans and low rates.

Term Universal Life—This is one of the most popular types of universal life policies. The policy covers your family for a specified amount of time (i.e., 30 years) and can be financed over that time period.

How to Open a Broker Account

Opening a broker account can be daunting, especially for a beginner. Beginners may not know what to expect and may feel bombarded by the myriad of options and possibilities when looking at different accounts.

What types of brokerage accounts are there?

- Regular Brokerage Account: This type of brokerage account typically has high trading fees and minimum payment requirements. These types of brokerage accounts don't come with any financial advice or guidance unless you pay for it separately.

- Discount Brokerage Account: A discount brokerage account has lower trading fees and offers more services than regular brokerage accounts. Discount brokerages usually provide financial advice as well as guidance on how to invest your money.

How can I tell the difference between a good and a bad broker?

Look at their historical performance chart. The best brokers will have the most recent performance data available, which should be displayed on their website. The data will show how well they have performed over time, as well as what kind of fees they charge for each kind of transaction you might make through them (trading fees, account maintenance fees etc.). Look at the minimum requirements for starting an account—some brokers might require larger amounts than others. Call up the broker and ask about their services. It's best if you can speak with a real person to get a feeling of how helpful they are and what kind of customer service they provide.

What should I be looking for when opening an account?

A good broker will display all available information on their website so you can easily decide whether or not it's the right broker for you. Look at the financial health of the brokerage firm—this is usually displayed on their website as well. You should look at whether or not they are a member of any regulatory bodies, like the SEC or FINRA. If they are a member of such bodies, it means that they have undergone a certain level of scrutiny by the institution. You can also look up their latest financial reports with the SEC.

Can I open an account without depositing any money?

Some discount brokerages will allow you to open an account without depositing any money—though some might require a little bit of collateral in order to provide you with the initial trading/investing tools (like a working phone number and email address). It's best if you can fill out your profile completely before applying for an account—don't leave any fields blank! This way, when you apply for an account, there will be less information required from you.

How do I fund my account?

You can fund your account by depositing money, via a wire transfer or by using a credit/debit card. Be sure to look at the deposit and withdrawal requirements for each type of funding method so you can make your payment in a timely manner.

What is the minimum amount required to open an account?

Different brokers have different requirements for opening an account—some require more than others. You'll want to look at the minimum funding requirements for the broker so that you can have enough money on hand when you make your initial deposit. If the amount is too high, you may have to get financing from a third party.

What are some of the pros and cons of opening a brokerage account?

The most important thing to keep in mind when deciding if opening a brokerage account is right for you, is whether or not you will be able to follow through with it. It's best to find out as much information as possible about these accounts before actually applying for one. Once you have all of the facts straight, you can decide whether or not opening a brokerage account is right for you!

Can they open the various accounts themselves or do they need a parent or guardian to do so?

Yes, your teen can open an account on his or her own.

Do they need a parent or guardian to add money to the account?

Yes. In order for the account to be funded, at least one of our members must act as a co-owner/co-applicant to the account and deposit funds into the joint brokerage account. This is because we check if there are no sanctions against trading, that means, if you have no criminal record in any country. Also, we check if you are not registered in any other brokers from which we receive reports that you trade with them. And only after all these checks is done, we accept customers to our company and fund their accounts.

Are there any limitations or facilities for teenagers who put away and/or invest small amounts?

Yes, there is a facility for teens to open a trading account. The account can be opened either in the name of the child or parent. Brokerage will be charged for interest credited on such accounts and/or other financial benefits.

CHAPTER 14 Best Investing and Micro-Savings Apps

Finding extra money to invest is often a challenge. The accounts offered by traditional banks are appealing because they require no deposit or minimum balance, but the rates are generally low and the fees can be high. Fortunately, there are apps that will help you make it much easier to invest and save more money—without the headaches of old-fashioned banking. This details some of those app options for investing and saving, along with what each of their strengths and weaknesses may be. These apps offer features like intuitive interfaces, automatic deposits, tax-free growth in states with low-income taxes or none at all, and debit cards for easy access to your funds. Hopefully this information will help you find a savings account that fits your goals and needs.

1) Acorns

Acorns is an investing app for people who want to start small in their investing adventures. What makes it different from other apps is that Acorns uses a round-up system to invest your money for you. That means you can invest any amount of money, even if it's just $0.25 left at the end of the day after coffee or something. All you have to do is link a debit card to the app and when you use it, Acorns rounds up any purchases over $1 and invests the difference into exchange-traded funds (ETFs). The Acorns app is available on both iOS and Android, and it's a great option for those who don't want to worry about how much money needs to be invested or where the investments are being made. Plus, it allows you to connect with friends to reach your goals faster. While Acorns is definitely one of the best investing apps out there, it isn't the best micro-saving option. The round-up system can sometimes take a while to get going when you're only investing $0.25 here and there. But if you have more than enough money to invest, then this might be a great way to do it without worrying about anything else but putting your money into investments that will grow over time.

2) Robinhood

Robinhood is a financial app that lets you invest in stocks and ETFs for free with no hidden fees. The app, which is currently only available on Android and iOS, also allows you to buy and sell stock for just $0 commission. All you have to do is sign up with your name, email address and phone number, connect your bank account or credit card (you can also connect a brokerage if you want), link your bank account or credit card, choose how much of your deposit goes into savings versus investments, and that's it. Your money will be in the market within minutes. The next step is choosing stocks or other investment options. It's relatively easy to browse through the available options and see which ones seem like good investments. The app provides a specific set of alerts that will let you know when you have made money in your investments, and it also lets you view your actual account (how much money is in it, how much interest has been earned on the deposits, how many stocks are being held in the portfolio).

While Robinhood definitely comes with its own set of advantages, there are some drawbacks. For one thing, it does not support automatic deposits like Acorns does. Plus it doesn't support micro-investing or tax-free withdrawals because of its status as an investment app. Also, it's not much of a micro-saving app because there is no option for automatic deposits. Overall, however, it's pretty high on our list of the best investing and micro-savings apps.

3) Qapital

Qapital is an app that works as both a micro-saving and investing tool. It automatically transfers money from your checking account to a "virtual" savings account linked to the app and then invests that money in various ways. It offers easy access to checking and debit card functions when you need them, and it also supports automated payment options such as recurring monthly bills or paying yourself first for savings goals.

Qapital is a great option for micro-savings because it adds up your total savings amount over time and determines how much you should save. It's also a great investing app because it rounds up purchases when you use your debit card and invests the difference into one of its five investment categories: bank transfers, mutual funds, stocks, crowdfunding and charity.

Qapital is also host to more than just investing tools. The app also offers automated rules that will remind you to pay yourself first or save for something special. This makes it easy to manage your budget on a day-to-day basis while also saving money on things like recurring monthly bills. The Qapital app can be downloaded for free from the App Store and Google Play.

4) Acorns Spend

Acorns Spend is a feature that was added to the Acorns app in 2017. It's geared mainly toward people who want to save money for something special, like a wedding or a vacation, rather than simply invest money. It allows you to set savings goals, track your progress toward those goals, and set up automatic deposits so you can continue saving without having to worry about it too much or having to think about where your money is going. Plus, you get access to a debit card for quick access or payments wherever you need them.

Unlike Acorns Invest, you have to pay a monthly fee of $1.00 for the privilege of using Acorns Spend, but that fee is waived if you are a student or if you have an investment account with Acorns.

5) CapitalOne Investing

CapitalOne Investing is another one of the great options for do-it-yourself investors who want to choose their own investments and personalize each investment strategy for their specific goals. CapitalOne Investing allows you to choose from over 6,000 exchange-traded funds (ETFs), stocks, mutual funds and bonds available in its portfolio.

You can choose to invest automatically or manually, and you have free access to funds from your bank account. If you need help, however, CapitalOne Investing offers resources such as investment guidance and community forums so that you can get advice whenever you need it.

The Best Investing Apps

If you're an investor with no access to a financial advisor, but who still want to be in the market, these apps can help. They are all designed for people looking for a simpler, more hands-off way to invest and each offers different advantages. These are the best investing apps we've found.

These days, it seems like every app claims they can help you make more money with your investments. But can they? And are these apps really the best way to invest in your long-term financial goals? If you're a DIY investor with no access to a financial advisor, then of course, we recommend that you try to time the market. Seriously. You most certainly should.

But if you've tried and failed—and we know many of you have—then there are much better ways to make the most out of the money in your 401(k) than trying to time the market. These "best-investing apps" are designed for people looking for a simpler, more hands-off way of investing.

We review five options. Each offers a different advantage, and all you have to do is decide which best fits your needs.

Google's Smart Banking App

When Google unveiled its new smart banking app in July, the big selling point was multiple logins. That's the feature that set it apart from Apple's similar offering, which only works on the iPhone for now. But don't overlook the other perks—like ATM finder, balance alerts and even a budget-management tab where you can review your spending trends.

The Google Product Manager of Financial Services, Jonathan Alferness, told us it was designed for people looking to manage their bank accounts from anywhere. *"It's not specifically designed for high-net-worth investors,"* he said. *"It's designed for anyone who has bank accounts and wants access to them from anywhere."*

The Google Smart Banking App also provides market data to help you stay on top of the market with free real-time quotes and access to your latest account information whenever you want it—even when you aren't online.

Of course, the app can also send you alerts when your bank account balance falls to a certain level, or if there's an unusual transaction. The Smart Banking App is available for users of Bank of America, American Express, Capital One, Discover, HSBC, Navy Federal Credit Union and U.S. Bank. For now, it's mostly geared towards people with checking accounts—but Google will soon also offer savings-account and credit-card functions via the app as well. If you have a busy life—one that doesn't leave you with tons of time to monitor your investments on a minute-by-minute basis—then this may be the best investing app for you.

Fidelity Investments' Fidelity Go App

If you're looking to manage your investments from a smartphone or iPad, the Fidelity Go app is another smart choice. The interface is clean and intuitive—and it allows you to access your accounts on the go. Using the app, you can record your investment transactions, check up on their value any time of day and manage your cash flow from any location.

Fidelity also provides you with real-time quotes and charts, so you can stay on top of the market. And it's free to use.

If you're an investor with a number of different accounts, try to keep things simple by consolidating them all into a Fidelity account. Then just check the balances—and their progress—using the app. You won't have to worry about monitoring multiple accounts, or logging in and out of several different ones.

The Fidelity Go app is available for iPhone users. It works with any brokerage or retirement account at Citi, Morgan Stanley, JP Morgan or other firms that connect to Fidelity.

Acorns' Investing App

Acorns take the stock market out of individual investors' hands using its "spare change" investing app. It was designed so you can invest money in open-end mutual funds and real-estate investment trusts (REITs) through the app. All you do is connect your debit card to a FOLIOfn account and then set up a recurring purchase—every week, for example—for pennies at a time. Over time those small amounts have added up to some pretty impressive returns for many investors, including an annualized return of 8% over the last five years—with no account minimum. And if you want to begin investing, you don't have to set up an account or make an initial deposit. Just link your debit card. The app will automatically round up every purchase you make by a certain amount—typically a dollar or two—and put that money into one of five investment portfolios. The amount it rounds up is added to your investments but deducted from your balance. So, it doesn't cost you anything extra in fees. It's like having someone else investing for you so that one day when you find yourself financially secure, you can give back to others who aren't as fortunate as you are now.

Conclusion

The basic idea behind stock investing is pretty simple: to buy a share of a company you believe will perform well in the future. This means that the company needs to have a strong business or product, and it needs to be led by strong leadership. When a company performs well, and the stock is purchased at a lower price, you can sell the stock for more than you paid. This means that if your stock performs well over time, you make money.

The nice thing about owning stocks is that once they are bought, there's not much else to worry about: dividends will be paid out occasionally by the company, but that's not your concern; all you have to do is track whether or not your investment increases or decreases in value over time.

Sounds easy, right? Unfortunately, it's not quite so simple. One of the most frustrating things about investing in stocks is that it isn't always obvious what a company's share is worth. This is what we mean when we talk about a company's value (or stock price). The value of a company is constantly changing, giving investors headaches and making it hard to decide if they want to invest in this stock or that.

Is Investing in Stocks a Good Idea?

There's no one correct answer to this question. Some people are successful at investing and make a lot of money. In contrast, others lose out and don't get anything from their investment. Remember, a stock is only worth what someone else is willing to pay for it. If you have no idea how the stock market works or how much a company is worth, you can lose a lot of money.

So be smart about where you invest your money! If you're interested in buying stocks, you should do as much research as possible before making any investment. That means reading as many books and articles about investing as possible. It also means taking a class on investing if your school offers one. There are many different investing methods and approaches. When you start any new activity, you have to learn the rules to enable you to play the game in the best way. No matter how exciting the stock market appears, there is a certain amount of history involved.

There are several popular ways to invest or trade stocks, but they all involve some high-risk potential.

The first step in understanding the world of stock investment is to ensure that you receive a solid education on what both sides mean by terms such as "investing" and "trading".

To trade stocks means to buy them and sell them within a short period. The most famous example of this is when traders are in an unstable market. These investors use the stock market as a short-term replacement for income, essentially gambling that they can make more money within a brief period than it would cost to invest in the shares. The rule here is that the faster you sell your stock, the higher you will profit. The longer you wait to sell your investment, however, the more likely you are to lose out on potential gains.

Investing, on the other hand, is a far less risky method. In this instance, the investor profits from the company's growth over time. Investing in stocks is a longer-term strategy used to make money over several years or even decades. You can use the stock market to get some of the advantages of earning an income. When you invest in stocks, you are getting multiple cash over the years, with relatively little risk to your portfolio or your financial future.

The best way to be successful at stock investing is to keep in mind that it is only as risky as you allow it to be. If you put your money in safe investments such as government bonds and CDs, then your capital will not grow very much. This means that when you retire, you will not have much money left over. Suppose you want to make your money work for you and increase your capital. In that case, you need to put it in investment situations that are likely to increase in value over time.

Many stock investments will never go up in value. This is why it is essential to get the most reliable information available when you invest your money. One of the best ways to get information, and avoid scams, is to talk to someone who knows what they are doing.

The bottom line here is that there are several ways that you can invest your money for the future, but it always comes down to common sense and sound research. Don't ever rush into anything, and always verify that the investment is worthwhile. The sooner you start investing in your future, the better. Many people miss out on significant opportunities because they fail to take advantage of every opportunity that comes their way, and the stock market is a great place to make some cash. In order to get the best possible results, though, make sure that you educate yourself first.

We've talked in this guide about compound interest. The compound interest (also called "compound interest") is an amount of money that has been multiplied by the interest rate over time.

For example, if a person received 10 dollars from their bank account, and then the bank gave the person 5 % of interest on it, their new amount would be 11.50 dollars. The original amount of money is called the principal. Then, the amount of money after being invested is called compound interest.

On the other hand, investing at a young age brings many benefits:

1. **You will have a significant investment tool choice since you have more time to invest and gather more knowledge about how to make money by investing.** The reason for this is simple, when you are in your 40's or 50's, you will be focused on saving for retirement, your kid's education, or other things like buying a house or purchasing a car, and thus it will be much harder to learn about how to make money by investing and thus harder to save enough money for those goals.

2. **It will give you a head start in our global financial system.** Many of the people who become millionaires are simply the ones who started investing early, this is especially true in China since in our country there are many poor families that struggle to pay for their children's education and if you become rich earlier, it will be a lot easier to have your kids study abroad or attend an expensive private school.

3. **It will give you the power to make large investments.** If you are a young man or woman who is already making decent money, it will be much easier for you to make large stock and real estate investments. There is no doubt that making a single investment of

$10,000 is a lot easier than saving up this amount of money while having bills to pay at the same time.

4. **It will be easier for you to accumulate wealth since investing** in your 20's means that you have many years ahead of you to keep investing more, so even if your rate of return is just 10%, it can still turn into a considerable amount when invested year after year.

5. **It will help you build a network of friends who are wealthy and who will be able to help you get opportunities in life**. You might have a friend who already run his own successful company or is already a successful businessman, if so then this will greatly improve your chances of getting a job that pays you comfortably.

6. **Finally, you should always have a plan B for what to do if things go wrong**. If you're reading this, then that means that you're really interested in making money by investing and making smart choices with your investments.

There are some great opportunities for teens out there, but even those can end up costing you money if they don't work out the way you expected. Keep your goal in mind, but try not to rush - form your knowledge base and start building your future!

Bonus Chapter: NFTs Revolution

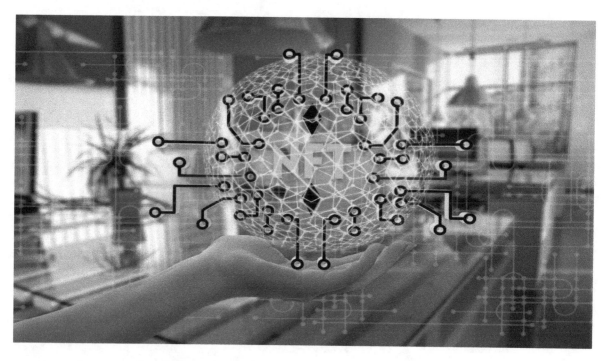

Today, non-fungible tokens are becoming more and more popular to represent digital assets.

In the past all digital assets were fungible. This means they could be replaced by other assets of the same type.

With the advent of non-fungible tokens, this is no longer the case: each token is unique and can only be replaced by another token that is also unique. This thing opens up a world of possibilities for the use of digital assets.

Non-fungible tokens have the potential to revolutionize how we interact with digital content and could have a significant impact on many different industries.

This chapter will explore what non-fungible tokens are, why they matter, and how they can change the world around us.

What are non-fungible tokens (NFTs)?

Non-fungible tokens (NFTs) are special cryptographic tokens representing ownership over an individual asset, often used to describe digital assets or collectibles.

Nevertheless, NFTs couldn't exist without a blockchain.

A blockchain is a shared and encrypted digital ledger where data transactions are stored, which in this way, becomes practically impossible to alter, manipulate, or delete. It is a system that guarantees the traceability, transparency, and verifiability of transfers.

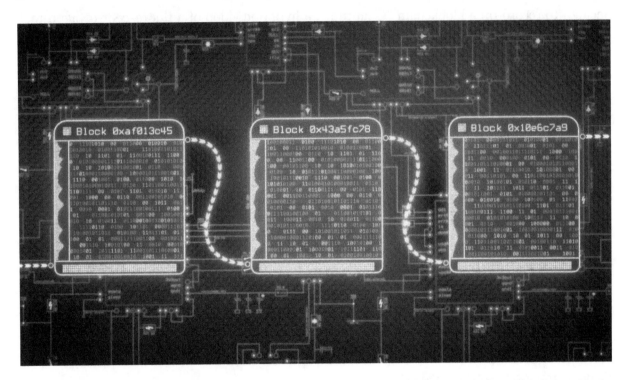

Each NFT carries with it its history that is defined by a string of numbers and letters called a "hash" that tells you where it came from and what kind of digital asset it is.

This code is generated using a cryptographic algorithm and is stored on the blockchain.

The hash allows you to track the asset's history and verify its authenticity. In addition, the hash can be used to determine the type of digital asset, such as a video, audio, or image file.

By reading the hash, you can learn about the asset's origins and identify any potential copyright issues. As a result, the hash is an essential component of every NFT.

For these reasons NFTs are unique identifiers (like a digital fingerprint) that cannot be replaced by another identifier of the same type, and they can represent anything from rare gold coins to collectible cartoon characters.

History of NFTs

Before May 2014, the word NFT did not yet exist. This is until the New York artist Kevin McCoy decided to record on a blockchain "Quantum", a hypnotic video of a fluorescent octagon that transforms into other geometric shapes, to search to monetize his work then put it up for sale.

Towards the end of 2015, the first NFT project, Etheria, was launched and presented at DEVCON 1 in London during the first Ethereum developer conference, three months after the launch of its blockchain. However, most of Etheria's purchasable and exchangeable tiles remained unsold until March 2021, when renewed interest in NFTs sparked a rush to purchase them.

Today, the most common means of creating tokens is the Ethereum platform, from which Smart Contracts are executed.

On this decentralized platform, developers design their applications or contracts on a custom blockchain.

In the Ethereum ecosystem, the tokens created are known as ERC-20. Non-fungible tokens abide by the ERC-721 standard.

How to use non-fungible tokens

Non-fungible tokens can be collected, traded, or used as a unique digital asset representing something else, such as a virtual object in a video game or an ID verification. The protocol also allows for creating decentralized marketplaces where digital assets can be bought and sold securely.

For all these reasons the main market in which the NFT's are growing the most is the artistic field, such as digital art, music, games, movies. Here below we will list some of the most famous examples in this context.

Some examples of NFTs: Crypto Arts

The most notable tokenization applications will likely come from the gaming industry, as it has been a major proponent of blockchain technologies so far.

A very famous example is "Cryptokitties", an online game that popularized non-fungible tokens in 2017. Just consider that, since the game's launch, users have already purchased over $23 million worth of tokens.

Cryptokitties is an Ethereum blockchain based game that, by using the NFTs, allows you to collect, sell and purchase virtual cats. This game has been developed by the Dapper Labs studio and it is the first great popular example of the use of NFTs as much that it was responsible for the congestion of the Ethereum network after a few months from the launch.

Since the continuous and exponential growth that this technology is generating in terms of offer and demand, it is clear that there is a profitable market that can be exploited in several applications. For example, since it is still difficult to find NFTs collectables a team of developers from Zynga built "Rare Bits" a marketplace that allows users to buy and sell unique digital assets that include anything from video games to virtual collectible cards, or even... Cryptokitties. In other words, this site is going to work as an "eBay" for artistic NFTs items.

Although NFTs are the most common blockchain application in the game industry, NFTs are not exclusive to games.

In the art industry, non-fungible tokens represent ownership or authenticity of the artwork.

Many artists have put their work on platforms like OpenSea, which allow people to buy and sell using cryptocurrency.

The NFTs are a new way for artists to benefit from an alternative to the traditional revenue model where they sell copies of their work and lose all rights to it after that copy is sold. Indeed, blockchain-based NFTs can guarantee a creator's rights to their digital work, allowing them to set terms for its use and collect royalties indefinitely.

In this regard, the strangest story involving NFTs is about Sultan Gustaf Al Ghozali, an Indonesian student who took pictures of himself every day for five years. His selfies, sold as an NFT collection, reached a trading volume of over $1 million in just two months! And he decided to do convert his selfies in NFTs because "it would have been fun"!

Even the music world could be use NFTs. Many artists are paid based on how many times their song is played by streaming services, which does not provide a good source of income because it doesn't consider how many purchases and downloads their music receives.

Individual musicians may use NFTs to develop a unique and limited digital asset and sell it directly to their fans. Every purchase permits them to download or utilize that song or painting, providing an additional revenue stream for creators who don't want to deal with intermediaries like Spotify or Apple Music or other music provider services.

Non-Fungible Tokens Games

As we discussed non-fungible tokens are gaining traction in the gaming industry.

NFTs offer a more immersive gaming experience and allow players to own and trade virtual assets in a secure and trustless environment. This could lead to new opportunities for gamers and game developers alike.

Some examples of games that use them include:

- **CryptoKitties:** This popular blockchain game allows players to collect and breed digital cats. Each CryptoKitty is unique and cannot be replaced by another token of the same type. The purpose of game is to collect as many different CryptoKitties as possible.

- **Ether Kingdoms**: Another popular blockchain game that uses NFTs is Ether Kingdoms. This game allows players to battle each other for control of virtual kingdoms. Players can also purchase and trade different kinds of creatures called Crypto-Creatures, which are also unique and non-fungible.

- **Gods Unchained**: Gods Unchained is a play-to-earn trading card game. Some of the cards in Gods Unchained are real NFTs that can be traded, sold, and purchased on Immutable X. In addition, the game asks you to link a Crypto Wallet in a special section so that the player can receive rewards on Immutable X.

- **Axie Infinity:** This is probably the most popular NFT game around at the moment. It is a digital pet community of creatives and collectors who come together to play and nurture adorable, battle-tested creatures called Axies. You can raise them, collect their offspring, form a team, and battle other players to earn Ethereum from each victory.

- **Sorare**: this is another one of the top NFT games currently running. Sorare is a fantasy world filled with monsters where you can hatch, raise, collect and trade monsters known as "Sorares."

In what other industries do NFTs have the most potential?

In case it was not enough clear yet, FTs have potential use cases across many different industries and many different parties can use NFTs for a wide range of applications.

For example, they could be used also for identity management (passports, legal documents, etc.), ticketing (concert tickets, airline boarding passes), real estate (title deeds), data storage (IPFS), or even (as you now can imagine) virtual goods in games.

Let's take some other example.

SelfKey uses NFTs to help users to manage their digital identity and personal data. This personal identification system helps people to define a safe for private digital data that may be used on financial services or to access to integrated systems or products.

Some experts believe that NFTs are likely to have the most significant impact in the marketing industry because of their ability to create unique digital assets tied to a single user. It could be possible to use these individual assets to create more personalized advertising and messaging, increasing ad revenue for companies.

NFTs may also impact the legal industry by allowing people to transfer property ownership without needing a third party involved. NFTs have the potential to revolutionize ownership by giving real-world value a decentralized platform for safekeeping and transfer of ownership. They also give developers greater flexibility in building their platforms since they can now create tokens representing tangible assets like rare collectibles or even hard assets like gold coins instead of random-access keys for online resources.

Another indisputable advantage is that NFTs could even help bring about more social equity by enabling transparent and fair marketplaces where users can trade items equally with those who created them.

What is the downside of NFTs?

One potential issue with NFTs is that they can't be divided into smaller units like traditional fungible tokens. However, many blockchain projects have already solved this problem by creating ways to split or merge these unique assets using smart contracts.

For instance, if you wanted to sell half of your CryptoKitty to purchase a new one, you could easily do that thanks to blockchain technology and its ability to facilitate peer-to-peer transactions without the need for any middlemen or third parties.

One other downside is that NFTs are still relatively new, so there's no guarantee of widespread adoption. However, the benefits of blockchain technology seem clear enough for forward-thinking companies to investigate how to integrate this technology into their business models.

For this reasons, it remains unclear which applications will catch on most widely and which industries will realize the most benefit from integrating blockchain technologies with NFTs. Hopefully, non-fungible tokens will continue to gain momentum as the use cases for this revolutionary digital asset type become clearer.

Ultimately, we have to talk about the environmental problems where NFTs are involved.

Blockchain technologies, including NFTs, Ethereum, and Bitcoin, have been criticized for their environmental impact, as the process of mining them requires a lot of energy.

The only process of mining Ethereum currently consumes more energy than the entire country of Chile. If NFTs continue to grow in popularity, that number will only go up. This increase in energy consumption has a real environmental impact, as most cryptocurrency mining still takes place on fossil fuels.

The large footprint is partially due to the many transactions involved with NFTs, including minting, bidding, canceling, sales, and transfer of ownership.

There could be other, greener ways of minting NFTs that don't require such a large energy footprint. One such method is called "proof of stake" (PoS), which rewards users based on their cryptocurrency ownership. This method doesn't require any mining and, as such, has basically no emissions.

The Ethereum community is in the process of making the switch to "Ethereum 2.0", which will use PoS as its consensus algorithm. If Ethereum 2.0 does eventually happen, it could reduce the energy consumption of NFTs by 99%. But until that happens, the environmental impact of NFTs is something that should be taken into consideration when buying or selling them.

What are the potential risks associated with using NFTs?

While there are many potential benefits to using NFTs, there are also some potential risks that we should consider.

One primary risk is that NFTs could be stolen or lost, resulting in the loss of the asset they represent.

Another one potential challenge for public blockchains is scalability — as more users join, transaction throughput decreases. This means that fees increase and transactions become increasingly slow and expensive. Public blockchain infrastructure must address this issue before we reach the mass adoption of NFTs.

Another major challenge for NFT adoption is user understanding of how blockchain-based assets work and decentralized applications' design and user experience. If no one knows about NFTs or how to use them, businesses or individuals won't widely use them indeed.

What are some potential uses for NFTs in the future?

NFTs have the potential to be used in a wide range of applications, including tokenizing real-world assets like art or houses.

They can also represent virtual objects like in-game gear or collectible toys. For example, players can store game items in their wallets and use them outside of the game to acquire other virtual goods with in-game assets.

In a future where NFTs are more common, online marketplaces could also list unique digital tokens for sale alongside traditional digital games and downloadable content.

Some experts believe that NFTs could be extremely valuable and even replace standard means of ownership in the future. One such example is car dealerships, where it would make more sense to own a token representing your car rather than maintaining possession of it. This would allow you to sell the token if you no longer wanted or needed your vehicle, even though you no longer own it.

NFTs could also be used in place of standard corporate equity, allowing companies to use tokens as an alternative to selling stocks.

It's possible that soon we could see a major shift in how we think about owning and transferring assets to other parties. It is even possible that the types of NFTs currently available are just scratching the surface of what is possible and may lead to more innovative uses for this technology in the future.

How can teens get started with using NFTs?

You can get started with NFTs by exploring projects that use them and learning how they work. You can also experiment with creating yours tokens and representing virtual assets or real-world objects.

Several online resources can help you to understand, create, buy and sell NFTs, and there are also plenty of forums and social media groups where you can discuss them with other users.

A tip: try to check out some Reddit groups: /r/Crypto Collectibles and /r/NFTs may be a starting point.

How Could you Know Where an NFT Came from?

There are a few key things to look for when trying to understand the provenance, or history, of an NFT. The first is to check the smart contract associated with the NFT. This contract should include information on who created the NFT and when it was minted.

Another essential thing to look for is a verified link between the NFT and its original source material. This could be a link to a digital file, like an image or video, or even a physical object that has been scanned into the blockchain.

Finally, it is also helpful to check whether a reputable third-party organization has authenticated the NFT.

These organizations can help verify that an NFT is genuine and has not been tampered with. By doing all of these things, you can understand an NFT's history and make sure that you are getting what you expect.

Conclusion

Over the past few years, there has been a lot of buzz around the concept of non-fungible tokens, or NFTs.

These unique digital assets can potentially change the way we interact with digital content, and many believe that they will become increasingly valuable in the coming years. While there is no guarantee that NFTs will become mainstream, there are many reasons why they are worth watching.

But one thing is for sure: NFTs are a fascinating development in the blockchain world. Their potential is huge, and we can only wait to see what comes next. So if you're interested in this new technology, be sure to keep an eye on it!

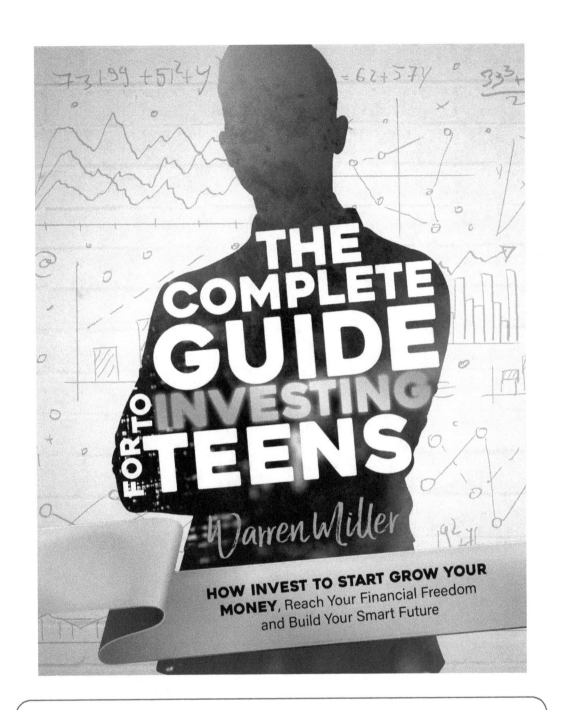

From the same Author

Available on AMAZON

CPSIA information can be obtained
at www.ICGtesting.com
Printed in the USA
LVHW061552051222
734620LV00007B/642

9 798506 403913

THE LAUGH AT THE END OF THE TUNNEL

MAUDIT TUNNEL BIEN-AIME

THE LAUGH AT THE END OF THE TUNNEL
MAUDIT TUNNEL BIEN-AIME

THE CHANNEL TUNNEL THROUGH CARTOONISTS' EYES

LE TUNNEL SOUS LA MANCHE VU PAR LES DESSINATEURS HUMORISTIQUES

Compiled by
Christopher Pick and enthusiastic members of Eurotunnel staff in England and France
Recueil compilé par
Christopher Pick et des membres enthousiastes du personnel d'Eurotunnel, tant en France qu'en Angleterre

With a contribution by/Avec la collaboration de
Pierre Daninos

Designed and produced by
The Public Affairs Department of Eurotunnel
Conception et réalisation
Le Service des affaires publiques d'Eurotunnel

Published by/Publié par
The Channel Tunnel Group Limited

First published in 1992 by/première publication 1992 par
The Channel Tunnel Group Limited
Code E280

Eurotunnel Exhibition Centre
St Martin's Plain
Cheriton High Street
Folkestone
Kent CT19 4QD
England

Centre d'information Eurotunnel
Boîte Postale 46
Chemin de Leulène
F62231 Sangatte
France

Translation/Traduction
Maryck Nicolas et Trevor Holloway, en association avec First Edition Translations, Cambridge

ISBN 1-872009-14-X

Printed by/imprimé par
Offset Impressions Limited

CONTENTS

TABLE DES MATIERES

AVANT-PROPOS
PREFACE

André Bénard KBE, Président/Chairman, Eurotunnel

Sir Alastair Morton, Chief Executive/Directeur Général, Eurotunnel

Le Tunnel sous la Manche est un grand projet qui enflamme l'imagination des chroniqueurs littéraires, économiques, techniques, politiques et aussi celle des humoristes. J'ai pour ces derniers une particulière affection. Leur imagination permet de s'évader d'un projet pesant et de rire un peu des problèmes en prenant de la hauteur. Contrairement à l'habitude, les dessous du Tunnel sont plus affriolants vus de haut.

La collection de dessins de ce livre comprend davantage d'oeuvres anglaises que françaises. La presse britannique est aussi beaucoup plus prolixe en histoires sur le Tunnel que la presse française : elle est plus abondante et elle raffole des histoires — et Eurotunnel en fabrique en grand nombre. Mais aussi nos amis britanniques adorent s'amuser et ils ont l'esprit cocasse. Un Premier Ministre Britannique visitant le Tunnel se réjouit comme un enfant à Luna Park. Une visite du Président de la République est soigneusement réglée dans tous ses détails par le Protocole et le Cabinet. Elle est marquée par la solennité. Les grands travaux vus de France ont un caractère quelque peu sacré ; les Anglais les ramènent à leur mesure humaine. Le Major Thompson rétablit l'équilibre.

La culture Eurotunnel fabriquera-t-elle des Anglais solennels ou des Français à l'affût de la drôlerie de l'existence ? Mes successeurs auront le bonheur de le découvrir.

Je souhaite en attendant une grande diffusion à cet ouvrage qui contribue à apporter à tous nos amis la légèreté qui rend distrayante la vie professionnelle tendue vers des objectifs difficiles et je félicite chaleureusement les auteurs et les inspirateurs.

The Channel Tunnel is a major project which has sparked off the imaginations of literary, economic, technical and political columnists and cartoonists alike, and it is for the latter that I have a particular fondness. Their imagination enables us to escape from the weighty issues by viewing the problems from a different angle, always showing us the funny side. Contrary to expectations, the intricacies of the tunnel are more seductive seen from another viewpoint.

The majority of the sketches in this book are drawn from English rather than French sources. Against its French counterparts, the more abundant British press, with its greater infatuation for stories, has produced a much greater profusion of stories concerning the Tunnel — and Eurotunnel is certainly providing a never-ending source of these. But in addition our British friends definitely adore being amused and have a mirthful nature. A British Prime Minister visiting the Tunnel rejoices like a child at Disneyland whereas a visit by the President of France is carefully set out in complete detail by protocol and the Cabinet; a very solemn affair indeed. Whereas the French view all major construction works as somewhat sacred, the British will reduce the whole thing back to a human scale. It is Major Thompson redressing the balance.

Will the Eurotunnel culture solemnify the English, and have the French always looking for the funny side of life? The pleasure of finding out I shall leave to my successors.

Meanwhile, I hope that this book enjoys widespread circulation as it will help all our friends discover an entertaining side to what is very tense business striving to achieve difficult aims; it is a precious gift for which I warmly congratulate the authors and the instigators.

André Bénard KBE

JAK, Evening Standard, 19 February 1990

PARIS 325 KM

⊠ ≠ BR — SCNF ▯
EUROTUNNEL
TRANSMANCHE LINK
COSTAIN, BALFOUR BEATTY
TAYLOR WOODROW
TARMAC, WIMPEY

JAK

"D'you know Wilson, I haven't seen a boardroom battle like that in years!"

"A dire vrai, mon cher Wilson, cela fait des années que je n'avais pas assisté à une telle bataille entre administrateurs !"

The Channel Tunnel will always be the 'Chunnel' to a generation that has watched its progress through the British subconscious from proposal in the early 1980s to reality in the 1990s. Future generations will puzzle over the difference in tone across a mere 35 kilometres of water: no one who has taken part in our progress, or observed it closely, finds it puzzling! It is the British way of absorbing some of life's less digestible new arrivals — to insult them, then to mock them and then, like the leaves on British Rail's lines, to make them our own. Eurotunnel, in this sense, has arrived — the cartoons are telling us that.

The cartoonists have had a struggle to distinguish 'our' project from 'the other one', the will-o'-the-wisp proposition for a high-speed rail link to connect Great Britain to the Tunnel. One can only agree, it's easier to confuse them — and if that has helped 'that Link' to progress in British understanding, that is good for Eurotunnel's shareholders!

Some of these cartoons are from my collection — I welcome this publication and, in enjoying them, wish every reader greater understanding of the adventure we are engaged upon, symbolized by the 'Chunnel'. Britain is backing into the twenty-first century and into 'Europe'. The grumbles and the jokes are our way of doing that. The cartoonists help us over the stickier points: they are essential to our progress.

Smith

"I thought it was a description of their Chairman's face."

Infos Eurotunnel Dernière Tranche
En partie marquée et en partie creusée
"Je croyais qu'ils parlaient de la mine du Président de la Société... "

Pour toute une génération de Britanniques qui auront assisté au plus profond de leur subconscient à la lente évolution du Tunnel sous la Manche, qui est passé du stade de proposition au début des années 80 pour devenir une réalité dans les années 90, il restera le "Sacré Tunnel". Les générations à venir ne manqueront pas de s'étonner de la divergence de ton de part et d'autre d'un petit bras de mer de 35 kilomètres ; mais quiconque aura effectivement pris part à l'avancement de ce project, ou l'aura suivi de près, ne saurait s'en étonner ! En effet, cette approche est caractéristique de la façon dont les Britanniques parviennent à absorber certaines des nouveautés les plus difficiles à avaler de leur vie de tous les jours — ils les insultent, puis ils s'en gaussent, et enfin, comme ils ont su le faire avec les feuilles sur les voies ferrées de British Rail, ils les adoptent à part entière. De ce point de vue, il ne fait aucun doute qu'Eurotunnel a accompli sa mission — les dessins humoristiques en sont la preuve.

Les humoristes ont eu bien du mal à faire la distinction entre "notre" projet et "l'autre", cette proposition évanescente en faveur d'une liaison ferroviaire à grande vitesse reliant la Grande-Bretagne au Tunnel. On ne peut qu'acquiescer : il est plus facile de les amalgamer — et si cela a permis à "cette fameuse Liaison" de gagner l'appréciation des Britanniques, les actionnaires d'Eurotunnel ne peuvent que s'en réjouir !

Certains de ces dessins viennent de ma collection — je me réjouis de la parution de cet ouvrage et j'espère que chaque lecteur en tirera non seulement du plaisir mais aussi une meilleure compréhension de l'aventure dans laquelle nous nous sommes embarqués, symbolisée par le "Sacré Tunnel". La Grande-Bretagne se fait tirer l'oreille pour rejoindre le XXIème siècle et l'"Europe". Elle bougonne et elle ironise, mais déjà elle commence à se faire à cette idée. Et ce sont les humoristes qui nous aident à dépasser nos réticences : ils nous sont essentiels si nous voulons aller de l'avant.

Sir Alastair Morton

"So, when's the end of the tunnel?!"
"Shut up and dig!"

INTRODUCTION

For long enough, even the most ardent advocate of the benefits of a Channel Tunnel had to admit that it was something of a joke. In both France and Britain, almost two centuries of schemes and discussions, and no fewer than three trial excavations, had failed to produce any tangible results. No matter how convincingly the case for creating a physical link between Britain and the European mainland was made, the tunnel seemed destined to remain a perpetual pipe-dream.

In Britain, the spirit of that well-known *Times* headline — 'Fog in Channel, Continent Isolated' — always prevailed. Over the years, opponents of a tunnel marshalled a variety of arguments. It would cost too much. It would compromise Britain's military security as an island fortress and offer an easy invasion route. It would be impossible to construct and, if ever it were built, unpleasant to travel through. And, underlying all these objections, a tunnel would violate the integrity and character of a nation whose traditional links with its far-flung overseas Empire were more significant than its commercial ties with continental Europe.

Now, in the early 1990s, the appeal of these arguments has at long last largely fallen away. Britain's political and economic future is inextricably bound up with that of its European Community partners. Trade with the rest of Europe is increasing, more British people are travelling more often to the Continent; some are even putting down roots there, witness the growth of second homes in France. And the tunnel itself, that joke of just a decade ago, has become reality and is well on course for its planned opening in June 1993.

The French, meanwhile, can be forgiven for experiencing wry amusement at Britain's belated and still not universally enthusiastic recognition of the advantages of the tunnel. Despite her equally proud and sensitive national identity, France, for all kinds of historical reasons, has never felt herself threatened by the prospect of the tunnel. Indeed she has always positively welcomed it on commercial grounds.

This major difference in national attitudes had a profound impact on the initial stages of the present Anglo-French project. Opposition came almost exclusively from the British side of the Channel, and much time and effort had to be devoted to meeting the commercial, political and environmental objections voiced there. One interesting side-effect was the frequency with which cartoons on a tunnel theme appeared in the British press. Cartoonists live off controversy, and so no significant landmark in the planning and the construction of the tunnel — and certainly not the project's well-publicized financial difficulties in 1989 and 1990 — has escaped their attention. For those working on the project, such interest has provided welcome light relief, and many of the cartoons that appear in this book can be seen on walls and noticeboards in Eurotunnel's offices in Paris and London, Calais and Folkestone.

French cartoonists, by contrast, addressing a readership less stirred by the tunnel, have rarely found it an appropriate theme: hence the numerical imbalance of French and British cartoons reproduced here.

By their very nature, cartoons are ephemeral and rarely survive longer than the newspaper in which they were published. The aim of this book is to preserve the best of those that have appeared over the years before the opening of the tunnel sweeps past controversies into the dustbin of history. Particular thanks are due to Pierre Daninos, who since the 1950s has entertained readers in both France and Britain with the exploits of the very British Major Marmaduke Thompson and his equally French wife, for giving us the Major's considered and, to our considerable relief, not too hostile reactions to the Channel Tunnel.

McLachlan, Punch, 29 January 1986

"OK, now here's the programme. The Channel Tunnel starts operating in 1993 —
we make 'The Channel Tunnel Inferno' 1994, 'Murder on the Channel Tunnel Express' 1995, 'CT' 1996..."

"OK, voilà le programme : le Tunnel sous la Manche est mis en service en 1993 — nous réalisons 'Le Tunnel Infernal'
en 1994, 'Meurtre sur l'Express du Tunnel' en 1995, 'CT' en 1996..."

Depuis bien des années, même les plus fervents partisans du Tunnel sous la Manche se devaient de reconnaître que l'affaire tournait au ridicule. En France comme en Grande-Bretagne, presque deux siècles de projets et de débats, et pas moins de trois excavations expérimentales, n'avaient produit aucun résultat tangible. Aussi convaincante que puisse être l'argumentation en faveur d'une liaison permanente entre la Grande-Bretagne et l'Europe continentale, le Tunnel semblait condamné à rester un semblant de château en Espagne.

En Grande-Bretagne, le sentiment traduit par la fameuse manchette du *Times* — "Brouillard sur la Manche. Le Continent est isolé" — a longtemps prévalu. Au fil des ans, les détracteurs du Tunnel soulevaient de nouveaux arguments. Le projet reviendrait trop cher. Il compromettrait la sécurité militaire de la Grande-Bretagne par la destruction de son insularité et l'ouverture d'une voie d'invasion toute trouvée. Sa construction poserait des obstacles insurmontables et, même si elle était menée à bien, la traversée du Tunnel serait un voyage des plus désagréables. Mais le motif qui sous-tendait chacune de ces objections était que le Tunnel violerait l'intégrité et le caractère d'une nation pour laquelle les liens traditionnels avec un vaste empire outre-mer comptaient beaucoup plus que ses relations commerciales avec l'Europe continentale.

Gray, Marketing Week, 1 March 1991

"C'est incroyable !! Te souviens-tu du temps où il nous fallait faire la queue pour embarquer sur un aéroglisseur qui mettait une demi-heure pour traverser la Manche ? Maintenant, il nous suffit de faire la queue pour monter dans le TRAIN et nous arrivons de l'autre côté en une demi-heure seulement ! C'est vraiment FANTASTIQUE !!"

"C'est sûr ! Et tout ça pour seulement trois mille millions de milliards de livres !!!"

Aujourd'hui, au début des années 90, le bien-fondé de ces arguments a, pour une large part, enfin été réfuté. L'avenir politique et économique de la Grande-Bretagne est inextricablement lié à celui de ses partenaires européens. Ses échanges commerciaux avec le reste de l'Europe se multiplient. Les Britanniques sont chaque année plus nombreux à se rendre sur le Continent ; certains vont même jusqu'à s'y établir, à en croire l'augmentation du nombre de maisons secondaires en France. Et le Tunnel n'est plus la plaisanterie qu'il semblait être, ne serait-ce que dix ans plus tôt ; il est devenu une réalité et devrait être opérationnel en juin 1993.

Hector Breeze, Daily Express, 13 May 1986

"And it should speed up the arrival of pilgrims no end!"
"Cela devrait accélérer de façon marquée l'arrivée des pélerins !"

Parallèlement, il faut pardonner l'ironie amusée des Français devant les Britanniques et leur prise de conscience tardive, et encore quelque peu mitigée, des avantages qu'offrira le Tunnel. Malgré son identité nationale tout aussi profonde et tout aussi susceptible, la France, pour toutes sortes de raisons historiques, ne s'est jamais sentie menacée par la perspective d'un Tunnel. Certes, elle s'en est même réjouie pour des raisons commerciales.

Cette divergence marquée dans les attitudes nationales a eu de profondes répercussions sur les étapes initiales du projet franco-anglais. L'opposition provenait quasiment toujours du camp britannique et bien du temps et des efforts ont dû être consacrés à assouvir les objections commerciales, politiques et écologiques soulevées par celui-ci. Une conséquence intéressante de cet état de fait réside dans le nombre et la périodicité des dessins humoristiques publiés dans la presse britannique sur le thème du Tunnel. Les humoristes adorent la controverse et aucune étape significative de sa conception et de sa construction — et surtout rien de ses déboires financiers qui ont fait tant de bruit en 1989 et 1990 — n'a échappé à leur oeil averti. Pour ceux qui travaillaient sur le projet, cet humour a apporté une agréable bouffée de fraîcheur à leurs tâches quotidiennes et, à Paris comme à Londres, à Calais comme à Folkestone, les murs et les panneaux d'affichage des bureaux sont égayés par un grand nombre des dessins qui figurent dans ce livre. En revanche, les humoristes français, qui s'adressaient à une audience moins sensible au "phénomène Tunnel", en ont rarement fait le sujet de leur oeuvre, d'où le déséquilibre flagrant entre le nombre de dessins français et britanniques que le lecteur trouvera ici.

De par leur nature même, les dessins humoristiques sont éphémères et survivent rarement au journal dans lequel ils paraissent. Le but de cet ouvrage est de préserver les meilleurs de ceux qui ont été publiés au fil des ans, avant que l'ouverture du Tunnel ne balaie toutes les controverses d'antan dans la grande poubelle de l'histoire. Nous tenons tout particulièrement à remercier Pierre Daninos, qui a su divertir ses lecteurs, tant en France qu'en Grande-Bretagne, avec les exploits du très British Major Marmaduke Thompson et de sa très française épouse, pour nous avoir fait partager les réactions du Major, réactions réfléchies, et à notre grand soulagement, plutôt bienveillantes à l'égard du Tunnel sous la Manche.

Kipper Williams, Daily Telegraph, 13 November 1987

**Liaison Fixe
par Henry Moore**

MAUDIT TUNNEL BIEN-AIME
TUNNEL AND BE DAMNED!

Major W. Marmaduke Thompson (and/et Pierre Daninos)

Que je sois damné par le Tout-Puissant et lacéré par les léopards lionnés (ou les lions léopardés : on en discute depuis six cents ans) de l'étendard royal si je mens ! Longtemps, dès qu'il était question du Tunnel sous la Manche, je voyais sinon noir, du moins rouge. Aussi rouge que moi.

Dans ces tubulures souterraines, je ne voyais qu'un cordon ombilical attachant Miss Britannia au Continent en lui faisant perdre sa virginité. Je ne discernais qu'une atteinte à notre insularité, et une voie d'invasion.

Fallait-il que je fusse *old-fashioned,* et bête ! Mais Meredith ne l'assurait-il pas ? Il y a à peu près autant d'imbéciles en Angleterre qu'en France... Seulement l'imbécile anglais est un imbécile tout court, tandis que l'imbécile français est un imbécile qui raisonne. Du coup je me demande s'il y a encore en Angleterre autant d'imbéciles que je le fus. La réponse est "oui". A preuve ce dessin du *Times* paru mille ans après Guillaume le Conquérant, je veux dire en 1966 : trois hommes d'affaires très sérieux (y a t-il des hommes d'affaires comiques ?) y prévoient que le projet sera abandonné en 1971.

J'ai donc revisé mon jugement de vieux major coriace, mais je dois avouer que, bien souvent encore, là où l'on voit progrès et commodité, je ne trouve que décadence et inconfort. A l'instant où l'on traverse l'Atlantique en trois heures, j'éprouve un malsain plaisir à mettre à peu près le même temps pour franchir le Channel en bateau. Et au moment où l'on ne cesse de battre des records de vitesse, la lenteur m'apparaît comme un signe de fortune. Quant au silence, c'est le grand luxe.

Notre terre ne rétrécit pas seulement à vue d'oeil, et à coups d'ailes : elle rapetisse jusqu'aux mots. Il faut être rétrograde pour regretter l'époque où nous mettions les Indes au pluriel. Mais comment pourrait-on s'endormir dans l'Orient Express au rythme des somptueuses syllabes de Constantinople, quand Istanbul les a ratatinées ?

Alors... peut-on admettre qu'il existe encore en Grande-Bretagne quelques vieux crabes comme moi qui marchent à reculons et ne voient la vie que dans leur rétroviseur ? C'est bien possible, je veux dire : c'est certain. Car, aussi étrange que cela puisse paraître, chez nous tout a changé et rien n'a complètement disparu. Mon traducteur, P.C. Daninos, prétend que l'on pourrait en dire autant de la France.

En tout cas, à considérer les dessins publiés ici, on constatera très vite combien — anglaises ou françaises — certaines idées reçues ont la vie dure. Je condamne volontiers ma morosité passagère et suis devenu tout à fait pro-Tunnel. Je veux même oublier qu'en 1920 Lord Curzon, tout en prônant l'amitié franco-anglaise à propos de Tunnel, soulignait que "la Grande-Bretagne ne pouvait absolument pas compter sur la stabilité de l'opinion française"... Mais, si les temps ont changé, il n'en demeure pas moins, ces *cartoons* le prouvent, que les Anglais restent abonnés par les Français à *perfide Albion* et que les Français restent pour nous des *mangeurs de grenouilles,* quand ils n'ont pas tendance à "laisser des serveuses démembrées dans les consignes de la gare de Lyons" (*Lyon* avec un *s,* tant il est rare que des mots français soient traduits correctement en anglais, et vice-versa).

Hypocrites, *shocking*, perfides... les clichés les plus éculés traversent les siècles inaltérés, fidèles reflets de nos caractères nationaux, voire nationalistes.

Alors... rien de changé ? Si. Le temps est loin où Stendhal déclarait que les Anglais faisaient l'amour une fois par mois et, entre temps, s'ennuyaient. Un peu plus proche celui où mon aïeule Lady Plunkett chaussait de mousseline les pieds de son piano à queue. Elle trouverait notre société hautement lubrique.

Pierre Daninos m'a dit que, dans sa jeunesse, les enfants français symbolisaient la prude Albion par l'exclamation "*Oh... shocking !*" Au Bois de Boulogne, les gouvernantes anglaises, dragons écarlates à faux-col blanc et cape marron, faisaient régner leur *rule* en dressant les *badly behaved French boys and girls*.

Les *nannies* de Norland sont parties pour les USA ou l'Arabie, mais le terme qui revient inévitablement sous la plume d'un reporter français si un scandale éclate à Buckingham Palace, c'est : "*Shocking* !"

D'ailleurs, comment pourrait-on dire que l'Angleterre n'est plus prude puisque le Guide Michelin 1991, citant la *pâté de poulet froid au homard* de l'hôtel Connaught, l'accompagne d'une *sauce pudeur ?*

Veut-on de nouvelles preuves à ce que j'avance — cette fois sans reculer — en confirmant qu'ici tout change sans que rien disparaisse ?

Jadis, dans la bonne bourgeoisie française, on apprenait aux enfants à se tenir à table les coudes au corps "comme les Anglais". Aujourd'hui les Anglais mangent mieux mais se tiennent moins bien.

Mahood, The Times, 4 November 1966

"All dates are tentative at the moment, but we expect the financial backing in 1968, planning and execution of approaches in 1969, work on the tunnel started in 1970 and the whole project abandoned in 1971 due to escalating costs."

"Les dates n'ont rien de définitif pour le moment, mais nous prévoyons l'obtention du soutien financier en 1968, la réalisation des travaux sur les approches en 1969, le commencement de l'excavation du tunnel en 1970 et l'abandon du projet en 1971 en raison de la flambée des coûts."

Ce manque de tenue date-t-il de l'après guerre ? On pourrait le penser si l'on en croit l'auteur d'un ouvrage intitulé *The Rise and Fall of the British Nanny*. Jonathan Gathorne-Hardy décrit ainsi le comportement des *nannies* pendant le *blitz*.

"Souvent leur courage résultait de leur seul point de vue de nurse. Mrs Priscilla Napier décrit une scène qui se situe à Plymouth en 1940. Un bombardement aérien a lieu à l'heure du déjeuner. Un enfant de deux ans demande : "qu'est-ce que c'est que ce bruit, *Nanny* ?" — "Des bombes *Dear,* les coudes hors de la table !"

On voit par là combien les choses ont changé. Une *nanny* de ce type aurait quelque mal à s'habituer au relâchement des moeurs, et des coudes, comme au fait que les femmes en montrent dans la rue, à Londres, beaucoup plus qu'à Paris.

Cette permissivité signifie-t-elle que la Grande-Bretagne n'est plus un pays d'hommes ? Pas du tout ! Quinze ans après le *Sex Discrimination Act*, le *Marylebone Cricket Club* a renouvelé son veto à l'admission des femmes dans son *Pavilion,* et 85% de nos clubs de golf en interdisent le parcours aux *females* pendant le week end. Même en semaine, priorité est donnée aux hommes pour prendre le départ.

Ainsi vont les choses. Ainsi ne vont-elles pas.

Mais je voudrais revenir une nouvelle fois sur ces *cartoons* car, s'ils disent bien ce qui est parti et ce qui reste, ils montrent aussi la différence qui demeure entre l'humour anglais et l'esprit français.

Carlyle disait : "L'esprit rit des choses. L'humour rit avec elles." *That's true*. Esprit, ce mot de Capus répondant à quelqu'un qui lui avait annoncé : "Un tel est mort... On ne sait même pas de quoi !" : "Ça n'a pas d'importance, on ne savait même pas de quoi il vivait !" Esprit, cette flèche de Metternich murmurant (en français) devant un cadeau de fiançailles envoyé par Napoléon à Marie-Louise : "Le présent vaut mieux que le futur". Esprit génial, mais dont un tiers fait les frais. En revanche lorsque Saki déclare : "Je vis tellement au dessus de mes moyens que, pour ainsi dire, nous vivons à part", qui souffre ? Et qui souffre lorsque Oscar Wilde constate : "Je peux résister à tout sauf à la tentation" ?

Il y a tout de même des circonstances où nos trains du comiques se croisent dans le tunnel de la cruauté. Quand Sheridan écrit : "Au silence qui suivit je conclus que Lauderdale avait fait une plaisanterie" — il est rejoint dans son compartiment par Jules Renard qui parle à peu près le même langage en disant : "Il parlait très peu, mais on voyait qu'il pensait des bêtises".

Je ne voudrais blesser personne mais force m'est de constater qu'il y a plus d'humour au nord de l'équateur qu'au sud. Si l'on dressait un planisphère de l'humour, on verrait que les pays les plus ensoleillés ne sont pas toujours les plus gais. Plus l'on "descend" en Italie, plus l'humour devient tragique.

En fait, deux grands courants de l'humour proviennent de deux sources qui doivent bien peu au soleil : les Iles Britanniques et l'Europe centrale (le nombre d'humoristes anglais ou américains originaires d'Europe centrale est considérable).

On entend souvent dire, dans des pays qui ne vous font pas tellement rire : "Il y a un humour Papou !" ou : "Il y a un humour Esquimau". Je n'en doute pas. Mais, à partir du moment où les gens vous assurent qu'ils ont "un humour à eux", c'est que cet humour local n'est apte à courir le monde et qu'il lui manque le souffle de l'universalité.

Ce souffle-là, les Anglais (et les Américains) peuvent le posséder comme les Français. Quand Bernard Grasset, célèbre éditeur parisien, dit d'un auteur : "Il soigne son style mais il ne le guérit pas", tout le monde apprécie, comme tout le monde apprécie ce jugement de Samuel Johnson après lecture d'un texte : "Votre manuscrit est à la fois bon et original. Mais la partie qui est originale n'est pas bonne et la partie qui est bonne n'est pas originale."

Pour en terminer avec le Tunnel, et sans vouloir y rester, je crois qu'il ne changera rien à nos moeurs et à notre exclusivité : être le seul pays du monde qui permette de changer de planète sans quitter la terre. A titre d'exemple final, ce qui est arrivé, il y a peu, à Oxford. Les chiens sont acceptés dans la maison des professeurs, pas les chats. Un maître, nouvellement admis, ayant manifesté le désir de garder son chat, l'affaire a été soumise au *Dean's Council*. Après deux heures de délibérations, le chat a été fait *honorary dog*.

W. Marmaduke Thompson (et Pierre Daninos)

Walter Goertz

Major Thompson visite une demeure ancestrale anglaise.

Major Thompson visits an English ancestral home.

Entre l'Angleterre et la France, nous dit-on, rien n'a jamais été aussi mal — mais que pensons nous réellement les uns des autres ?
Sans regarder à la dépense, le magazine *Punch* a réalisé un sondage des deux côtés de la Manche.
Le 5 mars 1989, Miles Kington, créateur vénéré de la langue franglaise, nous a fait part des résultats.

CE QUE LES FRANCAIS ONT DIT DES ANGLAIS...

Ils sont toujours fauchés...

Ils sont arrogants (qui d'autre se permet d'appeler la Manche "le Canal Anglais" ?)...

Ils sont obsédés par les chiens...

Ils ne font pas de bons coureurs cyclistes...

Ils font de bien piètres amants (quand ils ne sont pas homos) mais il leur faut briser la glace de toutes ces cavalières frigides...

Ils se croient toujours les maîtres du monde, ce qui est complètement absurde ; la plus grande nation, c'est la France, bien sûr...

Ils parlent un français d'écolier si approximatif que personne ne les comprend outre-Manche...

Ils exploitent les jeunes filles au pair...

Ils sont toujours d'un calme olympien, non pas tant à cause de leur flegme mais plutôt du fait de leur inaptitude à faire preuve d'enthousiasme...

Ils adorent les défilés...

Ils ne peuvent pas se passer de ketchup...

Ils n'engagent jamais la conversation dans le compartiment d'un train, dans la rue ou même à la maison — ils ne se lancent dans de grands discours que lorsqu'ils rapportent une conversation confidentielle...

Ils n'ont aucun talent artistique ; leurs seuls génies sont quelques écrivains qui ont été acclamés en France et ignorés en Angleterre...

Ce sont des parents permissifs...

Ils chassent ce qu'ils ne peuvent pas manger...

Ils tiennent à ce que tous les étrangers parlent l'anglais et surtout pas l'américain.

Ils sont prêts à parier sur n'importe quoi (même la mortalité de De Gaulle)...

Ils ont de l'humour mais aucun esprit...

CE QUE LES ANGLAIS ONT DIT DES FRANCAIS...

Ils parlent trop vite...

Ils n'aiment pas les bêtes, sauf lorsqu'elles sont cuites...

Leur agriculture est arriérée...

Dès l'âge de cinq ans, ils sont perpétuellement dans un état d'ébriété contrôlée induite par la consommation de vin de table...

Leurs policiers sont ridiculement petits, à l'exception de Maigret, qui, de toute façon, est anglais...

Ils ont quelque chose qu'ils appellent haute cuisine : il s'agit d'un système qui consiste à masquer le goût des aliments avec de l'ail et des sauces...

Ils trouvent toujours de superbes excuses pour des performances médiocres...

Ce sont des amants endiablés, mais ils n'ont pas à se fatiguer avec toutes les femmes de petite vertu qui traînent partout...

Ils ont tendance à laisser des serveuses démembrées dans les consignes de la Gare de Lyon...

Ils conduisent leurs voitures avec la ferme intention de provoquer des accidents...

Ce sont des fripouilles qui se laissent guider par l'appât du gain...

Leur suprématie culturelle repose uniquement sur quelques impressionnistes, une poignée de poètes incompréhensibles et quelques ouvrages de Racine seulement étudiés à l'école...

Quant à leur force de frappe, ce mythe repose uniquement sur Napoléon (qui d'ailleurs était corse) ; ils ont perdu toutes leurs batailles depuis et ils ont toujours appelé les Britanniques à la rescousse...

Ils sont catholiques : on ne peut pas vraiment leur faire confiance...

Ce sont des parents tyranniques...

C'est seulement lorsqu'ils vont se coucher qu'ils arrêtent de brasser du vent...

Ils tirent sur les rossignols...

May I be damned by the Almighty and mauled by the lion leopards (or leopard lions: this has been a matter for debate for six hundred years) of the royal standard if I lie! For a long time, ever since talk of a tunnel under the Channel began, I saw, if not the dark side of everything, at least red. As red as myself.

For me, these subterranean tubes were nothing but an umbilical cord attaching Miss Britannia to the Continent and divesting her of her virginity. I considered them nothing but an attack on our insularity, and a possible invasion route.

Well, what an old-fashioned fool I was! But didn't Meredith say as much? There are almost as many imbeciles in England as in France, the only difference being that the English imbecile is simply an imbecile, whereas the French imbecile is an imbecile who reasons. As a result, I wonder whether the imbeciles in England are still as imbecilic as I was. The answer is 'yes'. And to prove it, look at this cartoon from *The Times*, published one thousand years after William the Conqueror, that is in 1966: three very serious businessmen (are there any funny businessmen?) predicting that the project will be abandoned in 1971.

So even this crusty old major has revised his opinion, although I must say that where other people see progress and convenience I still very often see nothing but decadence and discomfort. In an age when people cross the Atlantic in three hours, I experience a certain unhealthy pleasure in taking virtually the same time to cross the Channel by ferry. And at a time when speed

records are continuously being broken, slowness seems to me a sign of good fortune. As for silence, well that is the greatest luxury of all.

It is not only our planet that is shrinking rapidly by the minute: even our words are getting shorter. One would have to be an old reactionary to feel nostalgia for the time when the Indies were still in common use as a plural noun. But how can one fall asleep on the Orient Express to the rhythm of the sumptuous syllables of Constantinople, when Istanbul has shrivelled them up?

So... can we assume that there are still a few old crabs like me in Great Britain, who walk backwards and see life only through their rear-view mirrors? It's possible, indeed it's a certainty. For, however strange it may seem, everything here has changed and yet nothing has completely disappeared. My translator, P.C. Daninos, insists that the same can be said of France.

In any case, looking at the cartoons published here, you will very quickly notice what a hard life certain generally accepted ideas — both French and English — have. I willingly renounce my temporary moroseness and have become a committed supporter of the tunnel. I even wish to forget that in 1920 Lord Curzon, while extolling Anglo-French friendship on the subject of the tunnel, stressed that 'Great Britain could most certainly not rely on the stability of French opinion'... However, if times have changed, it is none the less true, as these cartoons prove, that for the French the idea of perfidious Albion is still very much alive, while for us the French are still a nation of frog eaters, when they are not leaving dismembered waitresses in luggage lockers in the Gare de Lyons (Lyon with an s — rarely are French words translated correctly into English, and vice-versa).

Hypocritical, shocking, perfidious... the most hackneyed cliches come down unchanged through the centuries, faithful reflections of our national, indeed our nationalist, characters.

So... has nothing changed? Yes, of course it has. The time is long gone when Stendhal said of the English that they made love once a month, and in between got bored. It is not quite so long ago since my ancestress Lady Plunkett covered the feet of her grand piano with muslin. She would find our society extremely libidinous.

Pierre Daninos has told me that in his youth French children signified prudish Albion with the exclamation 'Oh... shocking!' In the Bois de Boulogne, English governesses, scarlet dragons in their white detachable collars and brown capes, enforced their rule by taming badly behaved French boys and girls.

The Norland nannies have left for the USA or the Arab countries, but the word that French reporters inevitably reach for if scandal breaks out in Buckingham Palace is 'shocking!'

Anyway, how can we say that England is no longer prudish when the 1991 Michelin Guide, mentioning the cold chicken and lobster pâté at the Connaught Hotel, says that it is accompanied by a 'modest sauce'?

Do we need any further proof of the suggestion I have put forward — this time without going back on it — namely, that everything here is changing without anything disappearing?

In good French bourgeois families, parents used to teach children to tuck their elbows into their sides when at table, 'like the English.' Today, the English eat better food, but their manners are not so good.

Does this decline in standards date from the post-war years? One might think so if the author of a book entitled *The Rise and Fall of the British Nanny* is to be believed. Jonathan Gathorne-Hardy gives the following description of the behaviour of nannies during the blitz:

> Often their bravery was the result solely of their nursery-centric view. Mrs Priscilla Napier described to me a house just outside Plymouth in 1940. A day-light air-raid had just begun. The two-year-old said, 'What's that noise Nanny, what's that noise?' Nanny: 'Bombs, dear. Elbows off the table.'

This just shows how much things have changed. A nanny of this type would have some difficulty in getting used to the slackening of moral standards, and of elbows, and to the fact that women on the streets of London display a lot more than their Parisian counterparts.

Does this permissiveness show that Great Britain is no longer a man's country? Nothing of the sort! Fifteen years after the Sex Discrimination Act, the MCC has renewed its ban on women entering the Pavilion at Lord's, and 85 per cent of our golf clubs do not allow women on to the fairways at the weekend. Even during the week, priority is given to men when teeing off.

That's how things are going. Or indeed how they are not going.

However, I would like to return once more to these cartoons; if they show clearly what has gone and what remains, they also demonstrate the difference between English humour and French wit.

Carlyle said: 'Wit laughs at things. Humour laughs with them.' That's true. Wit is exemplified by this retort made by the French writer Capus to someone who had announced: 'Such and such a person is dead... They don't even know what he died from!' 'That doesn't matter', said Capus, 'nobody knows what he lived on!' Or by Metternich's shaft, whispered (in French) at the sight of an engagement present sent by Napoleon to Marie-Louise: 'Her present is better than her future.' A brilliant piece of wit, but uttered at the expense of a third party. On the other hand, when Saki stated: 'I live so far beyond my means that we live apart, so to speak,' who suffered? And who suffered when Oscar Wilde said: 'I can resist everything except temptation'?

Nevertheless, there are circumstances in which our comic trains cross in the tunnel of cruelty. When Sheridan wrote: 'From the silence which prevails I conclude Lauderdale has been making a joke,' he is joined in his compartment by Jules Renard who spoke almost the same language when he said: 'He spoke very little, but one could see he was thinking stupid thoughts.'

I do not wish to hurt anyone, but I do have to point out that there is more humour north of the Equator than south of it. If we were to draw up a planisphere of humour, we would see that the sunniest countries are not always the merriest. The further south one goes in Italy, the more tragic the humour becomes. (In fact, two great schools of humour have their roots in two regions that owe very little to the sun, the British Isles and central Europe: the number of English humorists and of American humorists of central European origin is quite considerable.)

In countries that do not make one laugh very much, you often hear people say: 'There is a Papuan sense of humour!' or: 'Eskimos do have a sense of humour!' I do not doubt it. However, as soon as people start to assure you that they have 'their own sense of humour,' it means that this local humour is not likely to travel the world, that it lacks the quality of universality.

The English and the Americans may very well have that quality, as well as the French. When Bernard Grasset, the famous Parisian publisher, said of an author: 'He looks after his style, but he cannot cure it,' everybody appreciated his wit, just as everybody appreciated this judgement of Samuel Johnson after reading a text: 'Your manuscript is both good and original; but the part that is good is not original and the part that is original is not good.'

To be finished with the tunnel, and without wishing to dwell on it, I do not think it will change our customs or our exclusivity one jot: we will continue to be the only country in the world that enables you to change planet without leaving the Earth. By way of a final example, I will relate something that happened a short while ago in Oxford. Dogs are allowed in college lodgings, but not cats. A new fellow expressed a desire to keep his cat, so the matter was submitted to the Dean's Council. After two hours of deliberation, the cat was made an honorary dog.

W. Marmaduke Thompson
(with Pierre Daninos)

Major Thompson strolls on the banks of the Seine.
Major Thompson se promène sur les bords de la Seine.

Walter Goertz

29

Anglo-French relations, we are told, are at an all time low — but what do we really think of each other?
At gigantic expense Punch has polled both sides of the Channel.
On 5 March 1989, Miles Kington, creator of the celebrated franglais, reported on the results.

THE ENGLISH SAID THAT THE FRENCH...

talk too fast...

do not love animals, unless cooked...

are agriculturally retarded...

live in controlled tipsiness from the age of five, induced by vin ordinaire...

employ laughably small policemen, with the exception of Maigret who is really English...

have something called haute cuisine, which is a system of disguising flavour with garlic and sauces...

provide superb excuses for poor performances...

are demon lovers, not that they need to be with all the easy virtue lying around...

have the tendency to leave dismembered waitresses in luggage lockers in the Gare de Lyons...

drive their cars with the deliberate intention to cause accidents...

are money-grabbing twisters...

have based their cultural supremacy entirely on a few impressions, a backlog of unreadable poetry and Racine's school-texts...

have based the myth of their fighting forces entirely on Napoleon (a Corsican), lost all their battles since then and always call in the British to rescue them...

are Catholics and not to be trusted...

are parental tyrants...

only stop waving their arms to go to sleep...

shoot nightingales...

30

THE FRENCH SAID THAT THE ENGLISH...

are broke...

are arrogant (who else calls it the English Channel?)...

have an obsession with dogs...

make poor racing cyclists...

are blundering lovers (when not queer) but have to break through the defences of those frigid horsewomen somehow...

think they are still masters of the world, which is absurd; the top nation is of course France...

speak 'O' Level French, a language unknown across the Channel...

are exploiters of au pair girls...

are calm at all times, not so much because of a stiff upper lip as an inability to become enthusiastic...

love processions...

live on ketchup...

never talk in railway carraiges, in the street or even at home — they only burst into speech when giving away confidential conversations...

have no artistic talent; their only geniuses are a few writers who have been hailed in France and ignored in England...

are parentally permissive...

hunt what they cannot eat...

expect all foreigners to speak English English, and not American English...

will gamble on anything (even the mortality of de Gaulle)...

have humour but no wit...

Oo eh der Goal?

Miles Kington and ??, Punch, 5 March 1989

TUNNEL AND BE DAMNED!

A GLANCE AT HISTORY
UN PEU D'HISTOIRE

Ever since the start of the nineteenth century, scarcely a decade has passed without some scheme being launched, in Britain or in France, for the construction of a fixed link across the English Channel. Visionaries and eccentrics, engineers, railway magnates, money men — their imaginations have been seized by the prospect of glory, and profits, to be won. For some, the creation of a fixed link became the ruling passion of their lives. Yet the same projects generated equally fervent counter-passions, above all among the British. French people, perhaps because they have traditionally regarded Britain as something of an off-shore island, have generally displayed greater equanimity. Cost and fear of a sneak military invasion via a tunnel were the two objections most frequently voiced in Britain. But these barely hid a significant element of isolationism, a belief that Britain's destiny should not be linked with that of continental Europe. Three times, in the early 1880s, at the start of the 1920s and again in 1973-74, tunnelling machines were manufactured and preliminary excavations were begun. Twice the views of the military establishment ensured the abandonment of tunnelling, while in the 1970s a combination of rising costs and lack of political will led to cancellation.

Bernard Partridge, Punch, 23 January 1929

THE CHANNEL CROSSING : 1929.

A RELIC OF THE INSULAR AGE.

BOY OF THE FUTURE. "WHAT'S THAT FUNNY PICTURE MEAN?"
MR. PUNCH. "WELL, YOU'LL HARDLY BELIEVE IT, MY BOY, BUT THAT'S HOW WE USED TO GO TO FRANCE IN THE QUAINT OLD DAYS BEFORE THE TUNNEL."

La Traversée de la Manche : 1929

RELIQUE DE L'AGE INSULAIRE

**Petit garçon du futur. "Que représente
ce drôle de tableau ?"
M. Punch. "Et bien, tu ne vas peut-être pas me croire
mais c'est comme ça que nous allions en France dans
le bon vieux temps, avant l'arrivée du Tunnel."**

Depuis le début du XIXe siècle, il s'est rarement écoulé une décennie sans que l'on assiste au lancement, en France ou bien en Grande-Bretagne, de quelque projet relatif à la construction d'une liaison permanente entre les deux pays qui traverserait la Manche. Visionnaires ou excentriques, ingénieurs ou magnats des chemins de fer ou tout simplement financiers, tous donnèrent libre cours à leur imagination, embrasée à l'idée de s'emparer d'un peu de gloire ou de faire fortune. Pour certains, la création de cette liaison permanente devint l'ambition motrice de toute une vie. Pourtant, ces mêmes projets soulevèrent des oppositions tout aussi passionnées, notamment dans les rangs des Britanniques. Les Français, sans doute parce que la tradition veut qu'ils aient toujours considéré la Grande-Bretagne comme une île quelque part au large de leurs côtes, semblent avoir su faire preuve d'une plus grande sérénité face à de tels projets. En Grande-Bretagne, les deux objections invoquées le plus fréquemment dénonçaient les coûts de l'entreprise et le risque d'une invasion militaire sournoise par le biais d'un Tunnel. Mais ce genre d'arguments cachaient fort mal un isolationnisme marqué, l'intime conviction que la destinée de la nation ne saurait aucunement être liée à celle de l'Europe continentale. A trois reprises, au début des années 1880, des années 1920 et, de même, en 1973-74, on assista à la fabrication de tunneliers et aux travaux préliminaires d'excavation. Par deux fois, la réticence de l'état-major des armées fit en sorte que le projet fût abandonné, tandis que, dans les années 70, l'inflation et l'absence de volonté politique s'allièrent pour contribuer à son annulation.

David Austin, New Scientist, 23 January 1986

"Je reste convaincu qu'il serait plus rapide d'attendre que la dérive des continents fasse son oeuvre."

Print published in 1803, at the height of the Napoleonic invasion scare in England. While the French are feigning invasion by both sea and air (the first cross-Channel balloon flight had taken place sixteen years earlier), the main attack is through the tunnel, of which the English are supposed to be ignorant.

Gravure publiée en 1803, à l'apogée de la crainte d'une invasion napoléonienne en Angleterre était à son comble. Les Français font mine d'envahir l'île par les voies maritime et aérienne (la première traversée transmanche en montgolfière avait eu lieu quelque seize ans plus tôt), mais en fait, ils lancent leur assaut principal par le tunnel, dont les Anglais sont présumés ignorer l'existence.

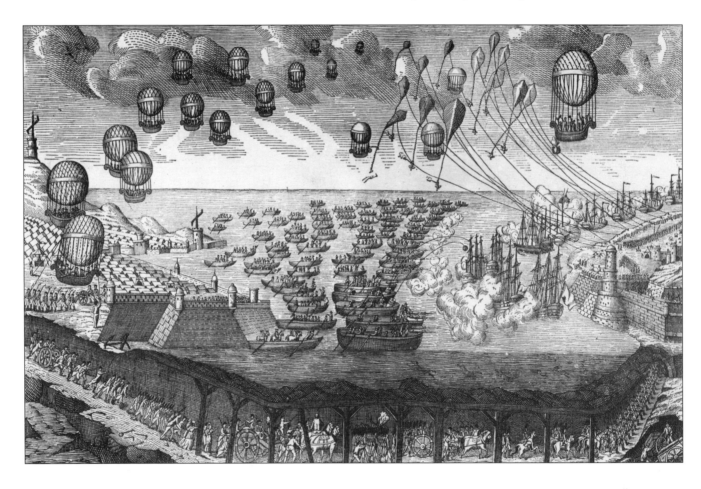

Mr Punch and the Tunnel

From its foundation in 1841, *Punch* supplied the British middle classes with a weekly diet of gently satirical political and social comment. Many of the magazine's cartoons were drawn by the most celebrated cartoonists of the period. The laconic reflections of Mr Punch summed up many contemporary attitudes; perhaps surprisingly, he often proved in favour of the tunnel's construction.

M. Punch et le Tunnel

Dès sa création en 1841, le magazine *Punch* a prodigué aux classes moyennes britanniques une dose hebdomadaire de satire politique et sociale au ton léger. Bien des dessins du magazine étaient l'oeuvre des humoristes les plus réputés de l'époque. Les observations laconiques de M. Punch résumaient l'attitude de nombre de ses contemporains et il est quelque peu surprenant de noter qu'il s'est avéré maintes fois en faveur de la construction du Tunnel.

Charles Keene, Punch, 7 August 1869

A PLEDGED M.P.

M.P.'s Bride. "OH! WILLIAM, DEAR—IF YOU ARE—A LIBERAL—DO BRING IN A BILL—NEXT SESSION—FOR THAT UNDERGROUND TUNNEL!!"

Stricken by a stormy Channel crossing, an MP's bride seeks her husband's support for Channel Tunnel legislation. In 1869, one of the first practicable schemes for a tunnel, proposed by two engineers, Thomé de Gamond and William Low, was under discussion by official committees.

Victime d'une traversée houleuse de la Manche, l'épouse d'un Député cherche à obtenir de son mari qu'il apporte son soutien au projet de loi approuvant la construction du Tunnel. En 1869, des comités officiels s'étaient vus confier l'examen de l'une des premières propositions de construction d'un Tunnel qui soit réalisable, formulée par deux ingénieurs, Thomé de Gamond et William Low.

UN DEPUTE ENGAGE SUR L'HONNEUR

Sa jeune épouse. "Oh ! William chéri — si vous êtes membre du parti — libéral — ne manquez pas — de présenter un projet de loi — pour ce Tunnel sous la Manche — dès la prochaine session !!"

Opposite: an immensely detailed commentary on the arguments for and against the tunnel produced in 1882 by Linley Sambourne, perhaps the best-known of *Punch*'s cartoonists in the late nineteenth century. In 1881-82, the Anglo-French Submarine Railway Company drove an exploratory 2.1-metre diameter tunnel 1,806 metres from Shakespeare Cliff towards Dover Harbour. However, work ceased in February 1882 following a national Petition of Protest, generated by popular fear of a sudden and unstoppable invasion from France, as well as sustained objections from the military authorities and an unfavourable report from a Parliamentary Select Committee. The 'timid hare' on the right of the drawing is General Sir Garnet Wolseley, who led the military objections. On the left are two long-standing advocates of the tunnel, Lord Richard Grosvenor and the engineer Sir John Hawkshaw ('old mole skin'), who had formed the English Channel Tunnel Company in 1872. At the foot of the drawing, John Bull is shown overcome by armed frogs emerging from the tunnel mouth.

Ci-contre : Satire particulièrement riche illustrant les arguments opposés au Tunnel et en faveur de celui-ci, réalisée en 1882 par Linley Sambourne, sans doute le dessinateur le plus célèbre de *Punch* à la fin du XIXe siècle. En 1881-82, l'Anglo-French Submarine Railway Company fora un tunnel sous-marin de 2,1 mètres de diamètre sur une longueur de 1806 mètres, entre Shakespeare Cliff et le port de Douvres. Toutefois, les travaux furent interrompus en février 1882 à la suite d'une pétition nationale de protestation, suscitée par la crainte populaire d'une invasion française soudaine et inéluctable ; cette pétition fut encore renforcée par les objections de l'état-major des armées et par la rédaction d'un rapport défavorable préparé par un comité parlementaire restreint. Le "timid hare" [lièvre timide] à droite du dessin représente le Général Sir Garnet Wolseley, chef de file de l'opposition militaire. A gauche figurent deux défenseurs acharnés du tunnel, Lord Richard Grosvenor et l'ingénieur Sir John Hawkshaw ('old mole skin'), fondateur de l'English Channel Tunnel Company en 1872. Au bas du dessin apparaît John Bull vaincu par une armée de grenouilles déferlant du Tunnel.

HOPES AND FEARS· OR, A DREAM OF THE CHANNEL TUNNEL.

Linley Sambourne, Punch, 25 February 1882

Espoir et Angoisse, ou le Songe d'un Tunnel sous la Manche

A contemporary American view from *Puck* of the Channel Tunnel arguments shows a fearful British lion, with General Wolseley on its back, fleeing the French cockerel.

Ce dessin, extrait de *Puck*, illustre comment les Américains de l'époque percevaient les différends engendrés par le Tunnel. Le lion britannique, chevauché par le Général Wolseley, s'enfuit, rempli d'effroi devant le coq français.

The American View of the Channel Tunnel Scare
Vision américaine de la vague de panique soulevée par le Tunnel sous la Manche

Garetz, Puck, 1886

The Lion can not face the crowing of the Cock

They might — flood it.

" brick it up.

" stand on the edge and chuck rocks down into it.

" blow it up with dynamite.

" put traps in it.

" load it with malaria.

" pave it with spikes.

" make it impassable by putting copies of the London *Punch* in it.

" pour boiling water into it.

" station a man with a hand-organ in it.

" put a *mephitis Americana* in it.

" cram it solid with the dropped Hs of the nation.

These are a few of the things which it has not occurred to the alarmed Britons that they might do in case the terrible French Army came marching in single file through a tunnel under the Channel, to emerge in England, one by one, and spread terror and destruction throughout the land. We might suggest a few other little plans; but these are enough to begin on. We confidently hope that they will be received in England with wild acclamations of delight, for the faithful people of the proud Monarch of the Sea are at present in a sad pickle of panic. The wail of the Wolseley is heard in the land and the poet-laureate rolls his five-guinea-a-line thunder at the impious heads of the would-be profaners of the 'silver streak'. The frightful and inevitable results of the building of the proposed tunnel are harrowing the British soul. The cool, clear British head has thought out just what would happen. Build the tunnel, and France, — our dear old bugaboo, France — will instantly declare war, seize the British terminus of the tunnel, and through that six-by-nine passage pour an invading horde into the helpless country. The voluble British tongue says nothing about what the unconquerable British Army and the invincible British Navy would be doing while these operations are going on; but what, after all, is cold reason, so long as the British heart beats true and fast?

Le lion ne peut supporter le chant du Coq

Ils pourraient — l'inonder.

" le murer.

" se planter près du bord et y balancer. des rochers.

" le faire sauter à la dynamite.

" y glisser des pièges.

" y introduire le paludisme.

" hérisser son sol de piquants.

" le rendre infranchissable en y empilant des exemplaires du *Punch* de Londres.

" y verser de l'eau bouillante.

" y poster un homme à l'harmonica.

" y mettre un putois d'Amérique.

" y entasser tous les H aspirés oubliés de la nation.

Ce sont là quelques-unes seulement des tactiques que les Britanniques en émoi n'ont pas réalisé qu'ils pourraient adopter si jamais la redoutable Armée française s'engageait dans un tunnel sous la Manche, en file indienne, pour refaire surface en Angleterre, à la queue leu leu, et semer la terreur et la destruction à travers tout le pays. Nous gardons bien sûr quelques tours dans notre sac ; mais un premier temps, ces quelques idées devraient suffire. Nous espérons vivement qu'en Angleterre elles seront accueillies par des tonnerres d'applaudissements, car il ne fait nul doute que le peuple loyal de la Maîtresse des Mers se trouve actuellement en proie à une profonde agitation. Les lamentations du Général Wolseley s'entendent dans tout le pays et le poète lauréat de la Couronne déclame ses vers tonitruants à cinq guinées la ligne aux oreilles impies des profanateurs potentiels de notre cher Canal anglais. Les conséquences inéluctables et terrifiantes de la construction du Tunnel proposé déchirent l'âme britannique. Les Britanniques, la tête froide et l'esprit clair, ont déjà deviné exactement ce qui allait se produire. Construisez le Tunnel, et la France — ce bon vieux croque-mitaine de toujours — la France nous déclarera immédiatement la guerre, s'emparera du terminal britannique, et par cet orifice de six pieds sur neuf dégorgera une horde d'envahisseurs dans le pays sans défense. Ces Britanniques volubiles se gardent bien de nous dire ce que feraient l'invincible Armée britannique et l'incoercible Marine britannique pendant le déroulement de ces opérations ; mais après tout, qu'importe la raison... pourvu que les coeurs britanniques continuent de battre haut et fort ?

Despite the increasing volume of public protest at the tunnel in Britain, work on the experimental tunnel under Shakespeare Cliff was not abandoned until July 1882. From the start of the 1880s until his retirement in 1894, the railway magnate Sir Edward Watkin was the leading British advocate of the Channel Tunnel. A forthright man of immense energy, he was Chairman of several railway companies (including the South Eastern Railway, which owned the Folkestone-Dover line that ran at the foot of Shakespeare Cliff), and also Member of Parliament for Hythe, just along the coast from Folkestone. As part of his campaign, he entertained fellow-MPs and other guests to champagne in the tunnel.

Malgré la montée des protestations du public britannique à l'encontre du Tunnel, l'excavation du Tunnel expérimental sous la falaise de Shakespeare Cliff ne fut abandonnée qu'en juillet 1882. Dès le début des années 1880 et jusqu'à sa retraite, en 1894, le magnat des chemins de fer, Sir Edward Watkin, fut le défenseur britannique le plus fervent du Tunnel sous la Manche. Homme d'une intense vitalité au franc-parler légendaire, il était président de plusieurs compagnies de chemins de fer (y compris la South Eastern Railway, qui exploitait la ligne Folkestone-Douvres au pied de Shakespeare Cliff), et député de la ville de Hythe, à quelques kilomètres de Folkestone. Dans le cadre de sa campagne, il invita ses confrères du parlement et d'autres hôtes à sabler le champagne dans le Tunnel.

Linley Sambourne, Punch, 15 July 1882

RULE BRITANNIA.

Britannia (to Sir E. Watkin). As I Rule the Waves, I must Draw the Line Somewhere, so I stop it at Channel Tunnels—till further notice. But happy to come and lunch with you any day and talk it over.

RULE BRITANNIA

Britannia (à Sir E. Watkin).

"Puisque je suis maîtresse des mers, je dois bien imposer une limite quelque part, et je ne saurais tolérer les Tunnels sous la Manche - jusqu'à nouvel ordre. Mais je me ferai toujours un plaisir de venir déjeuner avec vous pour en débattre."

In 1888, Linley Sambourne portrayed Sir Edward Watkin as the spider and the Liberal politician W. E. Gladstone as the fly in a mocking version of the English nursery rhyme. Watkin and Gladstone were close friends and political associates. Watkin extended a branch line to Hawarden, Gladstone's country home in Cheshire, and occasionally arranged his holidays abroad. In 1890, Gladstone repaid him by making a powerful parliamentary speech in support of an unsuccessful motion to permit tunnel excavations to be restarted.

En 1888, Linley Sambourne dépeint Sir Edward Watkin sous les traits d'une araignée et le politicien libéral W.E. Gladstone sous ceux d'une mouche, s'inspirant d'une célèbre poésie enfantine qu'il arrange à sa façon. En plus de leur association politique, Watkin et Gladstone étaient amis intimes. Watkin prolongea une ligne de chemin de fer de façon à ce qu'elle desserve Hawarden, lieu de résidence de Gladstone dans le Cheshire au nord-ouest de l'Angleterre et organisa de temps à autres ses vacances à l'étranger. En 1890, Gladstone lui rendit la pareille en prononçant, devant le parlement, un discours énergique en faveur d'une motion rejetée prônant la reprise des travaux d'excavation du tunnel.

THE WATKIN SPIDER AND THE GLADSTONE FLY (New Version)

L'ARAIGNEE WATKIN ET LA MOUCHE GLADSTONE (Nouvelle Version)

Linley Sambourne, Punch, 30 June 1888

"WILL you walk into my Tunnel?" said the Spider to the Fly,
"'Tis the handiest little Tunnel that ever you did spy.
You've only got to pop your head inside and peep, no more,
And you'll see a many curious things you never saw before.
Will you, will you, will you, will you, walk in, Grand Old Fly?"

Now, this particular Grand Old Fly *was* very "fly," you know,
And had clear business notions and ideas of *quid pro quo.*
Says he, "About your Tunnel patriots doubt, alarmists chafe;
Of course, it's most ridiculous, but *will you swear it's safe?*
Oh, will you, will you, will you, will you?" said the Grand Old Fly.

Said the Spider to the Fly, "It's most absurd, upon my soul,
To see so big a nation scared about so small a hole.
To share the scare that's in the air is worthy, don't you know,
Not of a Grand Old Fly like you, but of a midge like JOE!
Then won't you, won't you, won't you, won't you, plucky Grand Old Fly?"

"Will you show the feather white and vote with JOSEPH, Grand Old Fly?"
"No, if I do, may I be shot! It may be, by-and-by,
I'll ask you—but no matter; with you now my lot is cast."
The Spider laughed, "Ha, ha! my boy, I've got you safe at last!
You will then, will then, will then, will then, really Grand Old Fly!"

43

E. T. Reed, Punch, 28 March 1891

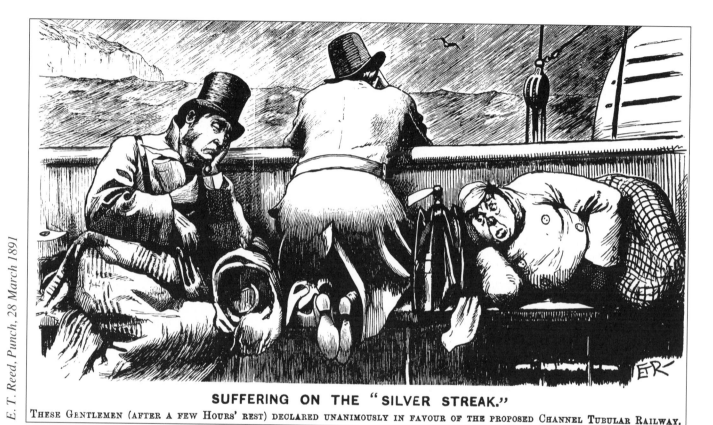

SUFFERING ON THE "SILVER STREAK."
THESE GENTLEMEN (AFTER A FEW HOURS' REST) DECLARED UNANIMOUSLY IN FAVOUR OF THE PROPOSED CHANNEL TUBULAR RAILWAY.

NAUSEE SUR LA MANCHE
Ces Messieurs (après quelques heures de repos) se sont déclarés unanimement favorables au projet de tunnel ferroviaire tubulaire sous la Manche.

Above and opposite: poor weather and rough seas in the Channel provided persuasive arguments in favour of the tunnel. Another, for French visitors at least, was the poor weather they suffered on arrival.

Ci-dessus et ci-contre : les intempéries et les traversées souvent agitées de la Manche offraient des arguments fort convaincants en faveur de la construction du Tunnel. Un autre argument, du moins pour les visiteurs français, était le mauvais temps qu'il leur fallait subir dès leur arrivée.

C. Harrison, Punch, 23 January 1897

Mr. Dibbles (at Balham). "AH, THE OLD CHANNEL TUNNEL SCHEME KNOCKED ON THE HEAD AT LAST ! GOOD JOB TOO ! MAD-HEADED PROJECT — BEASTLY UN-PATRIOTIC TOO !"

Mr. Dibbles (en route for Paris. Sea choppy). "CHANNEL TUNNEL NOT A BAD IDEA. ENTIRE JOUR-NEY TO PARIS BY TRAIN. GRAND SCHEME ! ENGLISH PEOPLE BACK-WARD IN THESE KIND OF THINGS. STEWARD !" [Goes below.]

M. Dibbles (chez lui, dans la banlieue de Londres). "Ah ! Ils abandonnent enfin ce fichu projet de Tunnel sous la Manche ! Et ce n'est pas trop tôt ! Une idée folle — et contraire à tout patriotisme !"

M. Dibbles (en route pour Paris. Mer agitée). "Ce Tunnel sous la Manche, ce n'est pas une mauvaise idée. Tout le voyage en train jusqu'à Paris. Un projet génial ! Les Anglais sont vraiment rétrogrades pour ces choses-là. Steward !" *[Il quitte le pont.]*

George du Maurier, Punch, 4 August 1888

OUR NATURAL ADVANTAGES.

M. le Comte (who has come to London for the Season of 1888). "AH BAH ! YOU ARE AFRAID OF THE CHANNEL TUNEL ! *QUELLE BÊTISE !* VY, IT IS NOT YOUR 'SILVARE STREAK' ZAT PROTECT YOU FROM ZE INVASION, *MES AMIS !* IT IS YOUR SACRED DOG OF A CLIMATE !"

NOS AVANTAGES NATURELS

M. le Comte (sic) (qui s'est rendu à Londres pour passer l'été 1888). "Balivernes ! Vous avez peur du Tunnel sous la Manche ! *Quelle bêtise !* (sic) Ce n'est pas votre Channel qui vous protège d'une invasion, *mes amis (sic) !* C'est votre sacré chien de temps !"

The year 1913 brought another burst of interest in the tunnel, and in early August a parliamentary delegation met the British Prime Minister, H. H. Asquith, to argue its case. The proposal was referred to a number of ministries, but, once again, military objections succeeded in prevailing.

En 1913, le Tunnel sous la Manche suscita un regain d'intérêt et au début du mois d'août, une délégation parlementaire rencontra le Premier Ministre britannique de l'époque, H.H. Asquith, pour lui soumettre un dossier. La proposition fut ensuite renvoyée à différents ministères pour étude, mais une fois encore, les objections de l'état-major des armées furent les plus fortes.

Leonard Raven Hill, Punch, 13 August 1913

THE ENTENTE TUBE.

STEWARD (on *night Channel boat*). "IF THEY BRING IN THIS 'ERE TUNNEL, MY JOB'S GONE."
MR. PUNCH. "THAT'S THE ONLY SOUND OBJECTION I'VE HEARD YET."

L'ENTENTE CORDIALE
STEWARD (*sur un bateau assurant la traversée de la Manche de nuit*).
"S'ils arrivent à faire accepter ce fichu projet de tunnel, j'peux dire adieu à mon travail."
M. PUNCH. "C'est la première objection valable que j'ai jamais entendue jusqu'ici."

Punch's portrayal of four former British Prime Ministers undergoing a practical demonstration of the benefits of a tunnel. The four — Lord Balfour (Prime Minister 1902-05), H. H. Asquith (1908-16), David Lloyd George (1916-22) and Stanley Baldwin (1923-January 1924 and November 1924-1929) — had attended a meeting of the Committee of Imperial Defence at which proposals for a tunnel had been discussed and rejected.

Dessin paru dans *Punch* illustrant quatre anciens Premiers Ministres britanniques qui se voient démontrer de façon pratique les avantages offerts par le tunnel. Lord Balfour (Premier Ministre de 1902 à 1905), H.H. Asquith (de 1908 à 1916), David Lloyd George (de 1916 à 1922) et Stanley Baldwin (de 1923 à janvier 1924 et de novembre 1924 à 1929) avaient assisté à une réunion du Comité pour la Défense Impériale au cours de laquelle des propositions pour la construction d'un tunnel avaient été étudiées et finalement rejetées.

MALAISE EN MER
M. Asquith. **"Loin de moi l'idée de sous-estimer le poids des objections de l'état-major à l'encontre du Tunnel sous la Manche. Pourtant, accroché à ce rail, j'ose affirmer, sans crainte de me voir contredire, que les arguments du peuple en faveur dudit Tunnel sont considérables, je dirais même indéniables."**
Les autres ex-Premiers Ministres (à mi-voix). **"D'accord !"**
Quatre ex-Premiers Ministres — Lord Balfour, M. Asquith, M. Lloyd George et M. Baldwin — ont récemment assisté, sur invitation, à une réunion du Comité pour la Défense Impériale, qui s'est tenue (sur la terre ferme) dans le but d'aborder la question d'un Tunnel sous la Manche.

Bernard Partridge, Punch, 9 July 1924

MID-CHANNEL QUALMS.

Mr. Asquith. "FAR BE IT FROM ME TO UNDERESTIMATE THE MILITARY OBJECTIONS TO A CHANNEL TUNNEL; YET, STANDING AT THIS RAIL, I ASSERT WITHOUT FEAR OF CONTRADICTION THAT THE CIVILIAN ARGUMENTS IN ITS FAVOUR ARE SUBSTANTIAL AND EVEN OVERWHELMING."

The Other Ex-Premiers (*faintly*). "AGREED."

[Four ex-Premiers—Lord Balfour, Mr. Asquith, Mr. Lloyd George and Mr. Baldwin—recently attended, by invitation, a meeting of the Committee of Imperial Defence, held (on *terra firma*) to consider the question of a Channel Tunnel.]

47

Heath Robinson and the Channel Tunnel

Originally well known as an illustrator of children's and gift books, from the late 1910s onwards Heath Robinson became increasingly celebrated for his humorous drawings of complex and improbable situations and mechanical inventions. Early examples included seven on the Channel Tunnel reproduced in the weekly magazine *The Bystander* in April and May 1919, which introduced the series in this way: 'Nearly every periodical has at one time or another claimed the Channel Tunnel as its own particular suggestion, and as time goes on will, doubtless, offer further suggestions as to the way it should be built. All that remains for us, therefore, is to give a hint or two as to the contrary how it should *not* be built.'

Heath Robinson et le Tunnel sous la Manche

Ayant fait ses débuts comme illustrateur réputé d'ouvrages précieux et de livres pour enfants, Heath Robinson devint, à partir de la fin des années 1910, de plus en plus célèbre pour ses caricatures d'inventions mécaniques et de situations inattendues et compliquées. Parmi ses premiers spécimens figurent sept croquis sur le Tunnel sous la Manche qui furent publiés par l'hebdomadaire *The Bystander* en avril et en mai 1919. La série fut introduite ainsi : "Pratiquement tout périodique a revendiqué, à une époque ou à une autre, le Tunnel sous la Manche comme étant sa propre invention, et au fur et à mesure que le temps passe, chacun s'empressera sans aucun doute de fournir des recommandations quant à la meilleure façon de le construire. Par conséquent, il ne nous reste plus qu'à formuler quelques conseils préconisant, bien au contraire, comment *ne pas* le construire."

The Channel Tunnel — Hints to Builders
Le Tunnel sous la Manche — Conseils aux Entrepreneurs

W. Heath Robinson, The Bystander, 2 April 1919

An Unaccountable Delay in the Channel Tunnel
Retard inexplicable dans le Tunnel sous la Manche

The Channel Tunnel — Hints to Builders
Le Tunnel sous la Manche — Conseils aux Entrepreneurs

W. Heath Robinson, The Bystander, 9 April 1919

A Nasty Accident
Quelle tuile !

Secret History of the Channel Tunnel
Si l'histoire du Tunnel sous la Manche m'était contée

W. Heath Robinson, The Bystander, 16 April 1919

An Early Experiment of the Inventor
Première tentative expérimentale de l'inventeur

UN PEU D'HISTOIRE

49

The Channel Tunnel — Hints to Aldermen
Le Tunnel sous la Manche — Conseils aux élus locaux

W. Heath Robinson, The Bystander, 23 April 1919

**A Well-known Magnate of the Port of Dover Laying
the Foundation Stone of the Tunnel in the Channel**

**Une personnalité du Port de Douvres pose la
première pierre du Tunnel sous la Manche**

The Channel Tunnel — Hints to the Navy
Le Tunnel sous la Manche — Conseils aux gars de la Marine

W. Heath Robinson, The Bystander, 30 April 1919

**Another Unfortunate Disaster — due to
Absent-mindedness of a Submarine Commander**

**Nouveau désastre regrettable — causé par un
capitaine de sous-marin distrait**

The Channel Tunnel — Hints to Passengers
Le Tunnel sous la Manche — Conseils aux Passagers

W. Heath Robinson, The Bystander, 14 May 1919

A Loose Brick in the Tunnel Roof
Défaut dans le revêtement du Tunnel

The Channel Tunnel — Hints to Engine-Drivers
Le Tunnel sous la Manche — Conseils aux Chefs de Train

W. Heath Robinson, The Bystander, 28 May 1919

Heroic Endeavour of an Engine-Driver to Stop a Leak
Tentative héroïque d'un chef de train dans le but de colmater une fuite

The early 1970s brought renewed hopes for the construction of the Channel Tunnel. Below: Garland shows Prime Minister Edward Heath proclaiming several costly construction projects. Geoffrey Rippon, Secretary of State for the Environment, is working at drawings of the third London airport at Maplin Sands on the Essex coast (later cancelled) and of the Channel Tunnel, while behind are plans for the Anglo-French Concorde supersonic airliner (built at well over forecast cost). In the background, examining plans for the budget, is Anthony Barber, Chancellor of the Exchequer.

Le début des années 1970 voit poindre l'aube d'un nouvel espoir pour les défenseurs du Tunnel sous la Manche.
Ci-dessous : Garland illustre le Premier Ministre Edward Heath annonçant plusieurs projets de construction onéreux. Geoffrey Rippon, le Secrétaire d'Etat à l'Environnement, travaille sur les plans du troisième aéroport de Londres à Maplin Sands (projet qui fut par la suite abandonné) et sur les plans du Tunnel sous la Manche, tandis qu'en retrait, on aperçoit les plans du Concorde, fameux supersonique anglo-français (dont le coût définitif dépassa les prévisions les plus extravagantes). A l'arrière-plan, Anthony Barber, Ministre des Finances, étudie des propositions de budget national.

Nicholas Garland, Daily Telegraph, 13 August 1973

"As a matter of fact we are also working on several incredibly expensive new ideas."
"Soit dit en passant, nous travaillons également sur plusieurs nouveaux projets des plus onéreux."

52

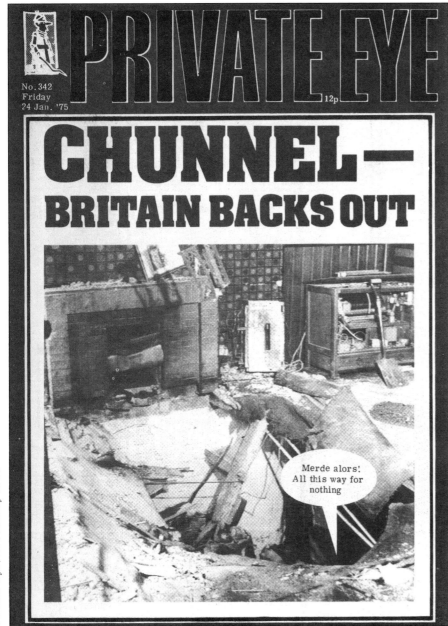

Private Eye, 24 January 1975

Front cover of the satirical magazine *Private Eye* following cancellation of the Channel Tunnel project.

Couverture du magazine satirique *Private Eye* à la suite de l'abandon du projet de construction du Tunnel sous la Manche.

LE TUNNEL SOUS LA MANCHE
La Grande-Bretagne se dérobe.
"Merde alors ! On a fait tout ce chemin pour rien !"

CONSTRUCTION

Although the geology of the Channel was relatively well known, and extensive preparatory survey work was done, the construction of the tunnel remained something of a venture into the unknown. This was to be the longest undersea tunnel in the world, and also the longest piece of underground boring ever achieved without intermittent shafts. The logistical problems were enormous. Everybody and everything — materials, equipment, ventilation — had to go underground at either the French or the British coasts, and then move along supply lines that finally extended for 20 kilometres. To begin with, tunnelling difficulties on each side of the Channel led to work falling behind schedule, and that had a severe impact on the project's finances. By late 1989, however, the initial problems were resolved, the tunnel boring machines moved into top gear, and a succession of tunnelling records was broken. Eventually, of course, the tunnels really did have to meet in the middle, and the prospect of their missing each other, and of mutual incomprehension when they did join, generated much humorous comment.

Newman, Independent Magazine, 8 December 1990

"Il fallait bien que ça arrive un jour ou l'autre !"

Mahood, Punch, 9 September 1988

"Looks like they're bringing in a new digger."
"On dirait qu'ils amènent un nouveau tunnelier."

Malgré une connaissance relativement solide de la géologie de la Manche et la réalisation d'une étude préliminaire détaillée, la construction du Tunnel n'en demeurait pas moins une sorte de bond vers l'inconnu. Il devait en effet s'agir du plus long tunnel sous-marin du monde et du forage souterrain le plus long jamais réalisé sans puits intermédiaires. Les problèmes logistiques à surmonter étaient gigantesques. Matériaux, équipements, systèmes de ventilation, et bien sûr personnel, bref tout, devait entrer sous terre, côté britannique ou français, et évoluer le long de galeries d'approvisionnement appelées à s'étendre sur 20 kilomètres. Au départ, des problèmes de forage rencontrés de part et d'autre de la Manche entraînèrent des retards sur le calendrier des travaux, ce qui eut de graves répercussions sur le budget du projet. Toutefois, fin 1989, les problèmes initiaux furent enfin résolus ; les tunneliers passèrent à la vitesse supérieure et l'on vit se succéder de nouveaux records de forage. En fin de compte, il fallait bien que les tunnels se rencontrent à mi-chemin, et la perspective d'un rendez-vous manqué et de l'incompréhension causée par les barrières linguistiques suscita bien des boutades.

David Simonds, New Civil Engineer, 19 December 1986

In the early days of the project not everyone was confident of its eventual completion. In its Channel Tunnel Game, based on the popular English children's game Snakes and Ladders, *New Civil Engineer* predicted a variety of difficulties and diversions.

Signature
d'un engagement à ne pas
faire grève — Avancez
de quatre cases.

Découverte
d'une taupe en
plein travail,
appartenant à
MI5 — Avancez
de trois cases.

Le Prince
Phillip insulte des
tunneliers japonais —
Reculez de quatre
cases.

...lier
...le
...creuser
...urci...

Une
épidémie de
claustrophobie
frappe l'ensemble
des équipes de
travail — Passez
deux tours.

Découverte
d'une ébauche
de tunnel datant
de Napoléon — Elle
vous sert de raccourci.

Découverte de l'épave d'un
cargo de Beaujolais Nouveau
— Votre gueule de bois dure
deux tours.

Le Prince
Charles crée la
Caisse de Retraite
des Employés du
Tunnel — Avancez
de trois cases.

Douche "écossaise" !
Vous vous réveillez pour
découvrir que ce n'était
qu'un rêve et pour
vous retrouver à la case
départ.

...e
...cile
...er

ARRIVÉE

Alors que le projet n'en était qu'à ses balbutiements, tout le monde n'était pas convaincu de sa réussite. Dans son Jeu du Tunnel sous la Manche, sorte de jeu de l'oie avec un seul dé, le magazine *New Civil Engineer* se fait oiseau de mauvais augure en prédisant toute une série de problèmes et de déviations.

Hector Breeze, Guardian, 1986

"When I was your age my grandfather showed me the preliminary workings, and one day..."
"Quand j'avais ton âge, c'est à moi que mon grand-père montrait les travaux préliminaires, et un beau jour..."

Another sceptical comment on the prospects of the project's eventual completion.

Un autre commentaire sceptique sur les chances de mener à bien le projet.

Plantu, Le Monde, 1er décembre 1990

"Even their air-raid shelters stretch under the sea!"

Mac, Daily Mail, 15 March 1988

"He says he's delivering a tender for the Eastern bloc's participation in the Channel Tunnel."
"Il dit qu'il est chargé de remettre une soumission pour la participation de l'Europe de l'Est au Tunnel sous la Manche..."

Above: a reminder of the grim time before the Iron Curtain was torn down and, opposite, Saddam Hussein puzzles over apparent undersea bomb shelters.

Ci-dessus : souvenir de jours plus maussades, lorsque le Rideau de Fer existait encore. Ci-contre : Saddam Hussein reste perplexe devant ce qu'il croit être des abris nucléaires sous-marins.

63

Dick Millington, New Civil Engineer, 1 March 1990

Millington's cartoon appeared soon after major management shake-ups in both Eurotunnel and the contractors Transmanche-Link during which several senior American construction experts were brought in to fill senior posts.

Ce dessin de Millington fut publié peu après d'importants remaniements au sein de la direction d'Eurotunnel et de son entrepreneur, Transmanche-Link, à l'issue desquels plusieurs spécialistes américains, experts en construction, furent appelés à assurer des responsabilités de direction importantes.

Bart, Guardian, 2 November 1990

Andrew, 1987

Simultaneous tunnelling from each side of the Channel gave rise to plenty of predictable jokes about the tunnels failing to meet in the middle. In reality, the difficulties of surveying such lengthy tunnels accurately were quite considerable. In the days before lasers and satellite technology, a fold in a plan could make a substantial difference.

Comme on pouvait s'y attendre, le forage simultané de part et d'autre de la Manche a donné lieu à bien des boutades sur la perspective d'un rendez-vous manqué. Les difficultés rencontrées pour contrôler la précision du tracé des tunnels aussi longs furent certes bien réelles. Avant l'avènement des lasers et des satellites, le pli d'un plan pouvait avoir des conséquences fâcheuses...

"I don't think he's allowing for the folds in the plan."
"Je crois qu'il n'a pas tenu compte des plis du plan !!"

Ridgewell, Punch, 24 March 1989

BERT, SHOW ME THOSE PLANS FOR THE CHANNEL TUNNEL AGAIN.

1932 caption – "HANG IT, ARTHUR, EVERY CUP OF TEA YOU'VE BROUGHT ME UP HAS BEEN PRACTICALLY STONE COLD."

"Dis-donc Robert, refais-moi voir ces plans du Tunnel sous la Manche !"
Légende de 1932 — "Mais enfin Arthur, chaque tasse de thé que tu m'as apportée était pratiquement glacée."

A modern caption for a *Punch* cartoon by Ridgewell originally published in 1932.

Légende d'aujourd'hui pour accompagner un dessin de Ridgewell paru dans *Punch* en 1932.

LAST EXIT IN NEW JERSEY — SPAIN THIS LANE

NOT TO BE OUTDONE BY FRANCE AND ENGLAND, THE UNITED STATES AND SPAIN BUILD A BRIDGE.

Se refusant d'être surpassés par la France et l'Angleterre, les Etats-Unis et l'Espagne décident de construire un pont.

More tunnel parodies. Above: the Americans build a bigger and better transatlantic link. Opposite: Heineken — whose beer is well known for reaching 'the parts other beers cannot reach' — proposes its own April Fool scheme for the tunnel.

Quelques autres parodies de Tunnel. Ci-dessus : les Américains construisent une liaison transatlantique plus performante et plus ambitieuse. Ci-contre : Heineken — dont la bière est bien connue pour atteindre "les endroits que les autres bières ne peuvent atteindre" — présente en guise de poisson d'avril sa propre version d'un Tunnel sous la Manche.

The Channel Tunnel.
Heineken submits its plans.

Le Tunnel sous la Manche.
Heineken présente ses plans.

67

JAK, Evening Standard, 22 September 1988

"If you want something done right, you've got to do it yourself!"
"Si on veut que les choses soient bien faites, il faut les faire soi-même."

Johnston, Evening Standard, 19 February 1990

CHANNEL TUNNEL

GATEWAY TO THE CONTINENT
THE EUROTUNNEL
COSTAIN, BALFOUR BEATTY, TAYLOR WOODROW, TARMAC, WIMPEY.

SITE OFFICE
ALL CALLERS REPORT HERE
NO SMOKING

"I'm sorry, that's what Mrs Thatcher's orders are — fill it up!"
"Je suis vraiment désolé, mais ce sont les ordres de Mme Thatcher : rebouchez-le !"

Despite her real enthusiasm for a physical link between Britain and mainland Europe, Mrs Thatcher proved a determined opponent of closer financial and political union. A favourite comment of hers was that to do a job properly you have to do it yourself.

Malgré son enthousiasme sincère en faveur d'un lien permanent entre la Grande-Bretagne et l'Europe continentale, Mme Thatcher s'est montrée farouchement opposée à une union politique et financière plus étroite. Elle se plaisait à déclarer à qui voulait l'entendre que pour qu'une tâche soit bien faite, il valait mieux la faire soi-même...

Eurotunnel : Morton pourrait bien changer d'entrepreneurs !

Kipper Williams, Daily Telegraph, 7 November 1989

ALB, International Freighting Weekly, 14 November 1988

Consortium of shareholders worried about the fines imposed for slow digging
Les actionnaires s'inquiètent au sujet des amendes imposées en raison de la lenteur des travaux

During the first year of construction there were some well publicized delays on the English side of the tunnel. On one occasion, soon after a European Disneyland had been proposed for a site near Paris, Alastair Morton, Eurotunnel's outspoken Chief Executive, threatened to dismiss the contractor. Here Disney dwarfs (but missing Snow White) set off for the tunnel face, while irate shareholders arrive to lend a hand with the digging.

Au cours de la première année de construction, des retards importants du côté britannique firent l'objet d'une publicité tapageuse. Ainsi par exemple, peu après la proposition d'un site près de Paris pour le projet du futur Disneyland européen, Alastair Morton, Directeur Général d'Eurotunnel, bien connu pour son franc-parler, menaça de renvoyer l'entrepreneur. On voit ici les sept nains de Disney (sans Blanche-Neige) se rendre au Tunnel d'un pas assuré, tandis que des actionnaires en colère viennent prêter leur concours aux travaux de forage.

"Nom d'un pétard ! On a dû prendre la mauvaise direction quelque part !"

Ainter, Le Parisien, 2 novembre 1990

"Them Frogs? They're okay if you like garlic!!"

Allen, Punch, 12 January 1990

"Are you sure you haven't broken through?"
**"Vous êtes vraiment certains que vous n'êtes pas
arrivés de l'autre côté ?"**

Media and public interest increased as the breakthrough
of the service tunnel approached, and when, on
1 December 1990, two tunnellers, one French, one
British, clasped hands through a hole in the rock the
celebrations were televized across the world. Cartoonists
used the breakthrough to satirize a variety of national,
and nationalistic, prejudices. Shortly after the *Sun*
newspaper, in an extraordinary outburst of xenophobia,
invited its readers one midday to turn towards France and
bellow abuse at the French, Ainter's tunneller recoils
from the stereotyped comments he overhears from his
English counterparts, while Allen's altogether more
sympathetic tunnellers have already adopted the long
French lunch-break. To their alarm, Warren's tunnellers,
opposite, have joined up with workers on the Sydney
Harbour tunnel.

Le tapage médiatique ne cessait d'augmenter au fur et à
mesure qu'approchait la jonction du tunnel de service.
Enfin, lorsque le 1er décembre 1990, deux ouvriers, l'un
français, l'autre britannique, échangèrent une poignée de
main par l'orifice creusé dans la roche, l'image fut
télévisée dans le monde entier. Les humoristes n'ont pas
manqué d'exploiter l'événement pour faire la satire de
toute une panoplie de préjugés nationaux et nationalistes.
Peu après que le journal le *Sun* eut invité ses lecteurs à se
rallier, dans un extraordinaire accès de rage xénophobe, à
une manifestation anti-française et à crier des insultes en
direction de la France, l'ingénieur d'Ainter a un
mouvement de recule lorsqu'il entend les commentaires
stéréotypés de ses homologues britanniques, tandis que
ceux d'Allen, à l'air plus sympathique, ont déjà adopté la
pause-déjeuner prolongée des Français. Ci-contre : Quant
aux ingénieurs dépeints par Warren, ils réalisent avec
stupeur qu'ils ont rejoint des employés du tunnel du port
de Sydney.

Jacques Faizant, Le Figaro, 1er décembre 1990

The French tunnelled under la Manche. The English bored under the Channel. That they met in the middle is nothing short of a miracle.

At the service tunnel breakthrough, rather than the two tunnel boring machines meeting head-on and creating a massive undersea traffic block, the British machine was turned to one side. David Simonds, opposite, depicts the resulting knot of friendship, or perhaps it is a Gordian knot, while, for Jacques Faizant, breakthrough is something of a miracle, given that the two nations even refer to the strip of water that divides them by different names. One of his workers has tunnelled under la Manche (literally, the sleeve), while the other has tackled the Channel.

Au moment de la jonction du tunnel de service, au lieu de laisser les deux tunneliers se rencontrer de front et créer un gigantesque embouteillage sous-marin, le tunnelier britannique fut dirigé sur une voie de garage. David Simonds, ci-contre, illustre l'amitié cordiale (où serait-ce le noeud gordien ?) qui en découle, tandis que pour Jacques Faizant, la jonction tient au miracle étant donné que les deux pays ne parviennent même pas à appeler le bras de mer qui les sépare par le même nom. L'un des ingénieurs a creusé sous la Manche, tandis que l'autre s'est attaqué au Channel.

David Simonds, La Croix, 3 décembre 1990

FINANCE
FINANCEMENT

"Je fais la manche parce que j'ai la moitié d'un tunnel à ma charge."

It is hardly surprising that cartoonists were quick to exploit both the twists and turns in the tunnel's financial fortunes and Eurotunnel's very public contractual disagreements with the contractors, Transmanche-Link (TML). In 1986/87, the Company raised £6 billion, largely from a syndicate of some 200 banks worldwide and flotations through simultaneous stock exchange listings in Paris and London. This was an unprecedented sum for a private-sector venture, and involved major publicity and promotion campaigns on each side of the Channel. Within two years, cost escalations (mainly caused by unforeseen tunnelling costs and changes to the specification of the shuttle rolling stock) were threatening to jeopardize the entire project. Negotiations with TML (about the apportionment of the cost increases) and the banks (for additional funding) continued during the winter of 1989/90 when, for several knife-edge months, the Company was bordering on insolvency. Later in 1990, however, the additional £2.7 billion needed to complete the project was raised from the banking syndicate, the European Investment Bank and a successful rights issue.

Il ne faut pas s'étonner si les humoristes se sont empressés d'exploiter les péripéties financières du Tunnel et les différends contractuels largement commentés d'Eurotunnel avec son Entrepreneur, Transmanche-Link (TML). En 1986/87, la société parvint à réunir une somme approchant 60 milliards de francs principalement auprès d'un syndicat de quelque 200 banques du monde entier et par une émission publique d'actions à la bourse de Paris et à celle de Londres. Il s'agissait là d'une somme sans précédent pour un projet du secteur privé et il fallut avoir recours à des campagnes publicitaires et promotionnelles massives des deux côtés de la Manche. Au bout de deux ans, la flambée des coûts (essentiellement provoquée par des frais de forage inattendus et par la modification des prescriptions techniques du matériel roulant des navettes) menaçait de faire sombrer le projet dans sa totalité. Des négociations avec TML (concernant la répartition des augmentations de coûts) et avec les banques (pour tenter d'obtenir des fonds supplémentaires) se poursuivirent jusqu'en hiver 1989/90 lorsque, après plusieurs mois sur la corde raide, la société se vit au bord de la faillite. Toutefois, quelques mois plus tard, les 27 milliards supplémentaires nécessaires à l'achèvement du projet furent enfin réunis grâce au succès d'une émission de droits de souscription et à l'intervention du syndicat bancaire et de la Banque Européenne d'Investissement.

Pesin, Le Monde, 6 septembre 1989

"Are you OK?"
"Oh! The usual lundi-matin feeling."

Matt, Spectator, 24 February 1990

Train électrique — coffret Tunnel sous la Manche

Dickinson, Financial Times, 23 October 1986

Nick, Independent, 25 November 1987

"Good evening — I'm selling onions to raise money for the Channel Tunnel."

"Bonjour Monsieur. Voulez-vous des oignons ? C'est pour une collecte au profit du Tunnel sous la Manche."

"Est-ce que j'arrive trop tard pour acheter des actions ?"

Opposite: French onion-sellers, traditional visitors to Britain, illustrate the project's changing fortunes. In October 1986 Dickinson reflected the difficulties the Company was experiencing in raising the necessary initial investment from institutions through a private placement. Little more than a year later, Nick's onion-seller was evidently alarmed by press suggestions that the Company's public stock-market flotation might be over-subscribed.

Ci-contre : Les humoristes se sont souvent servis des vendeurs d'oignons, image traditionnelle que les Britanniques se font des Français, pour se gausser des déboires financiers du projet. En octobre 1986, Dickinson dépeint les difficultés auxquelles se heurtent la société lorsque, par un placement privé, elle tente de réunir les fonds nécessaires à l'investissement auprès des établissements financiers. Quelque treize mois plus tard, le vendeur d'oignons de Nick est de toute évidence fort perturbé par les indications de la presse selon lesquelles l'émission publique d'actions de la société aurait donné lieu à une ruée d'investisseurs potentiels.

Dickinson's fairground Tunnel of Love was produced during the well-publicized dispute between the Company and the French and British railways about how much the railways should pay to use the tunnel.

Dickinson publia son dessin de la baraque foraine du Tunnel sous la Manche à l'époque du conflit entre Eurotunnel et les sociétés française et britannique de chemins de fer au sujet du prix à payer pour leur permettre d'utiliser le Tunnel, conflit qui fit couler beaucoup d'encre .

"I didn't realize that they were so strapped for cash."

"Je n'avais pas réalisé qu'ils avaient tant de mal à joindre les deux bouts !"

Dickinson, Financial Times, 1987

ALB, International Freighting Weekly, 20 August 1987

"He's in conference at the moment about raising investment funds."
"Il est en pleine conférence pour tenter d'obtenir les fonds nécessaires à l'investissement."

Although at times it seemed that Eurotunnel might have difficulty financing the project, the extreme measures suggested in these cartoons were never required.

"I'm from Eurotunnel in England, Mrs Trump — will you marry me?"
"Je viens de la société 'Eurotunnel' en Angleterre, Mrs Trump — Voulez-vous m'épouser ?"

Bien qu'à certains moments on se soit demandé si
Eurotunnel parviendrait à financer le projet, on n'en
est jamais arrivé aux expédients draconiens suggérés
par ces dessins.

"When le patron said dig deeper he was discussing finance."

"Lorsque le patron disait qu'il fallait creuser plus profond, il parlait finances."

Two reactions to Eurotunnel's announcement in early October 1989 of a substantial increase in the cost of building the tunnel and a major crisis in relations with the contractors Transmanche-Link (TML).

Deux réactions à l'annonce, faite début octobre 1989 par Eurotunnel, d'une importante augmentation des coûts de construction du Tunnel et d'une crise grave dans ses rapports avec l'entrepreneur Transmanche-Link (TML).

Keith Waite, The Times, 7 October 1989

Riddell, The Economist, 7 October 1989

Prolonged negotiations with the banks and TML on the project's future funding continued into 1990. These cartoons appeared the day before agreement was finally reached. At the same time ambulance drivers were holding street collections to fund their dispute with NHS management.

Les pourparlers avec les banques et TML concernant le futur financement du projet se sont poursuivis jusqu'au début de 1990. Ces dessins furent publiés la veille de l'accord entre les partenaires. A cette époque, les ambulanciers britanniques organisaient des collectes dans la rue pour financer leur conflit avec la direction des Services sociaux.

Austin, Guardian, 10 January 1990

"I gave it to a poor chap from the Channel Tunnel Company."

"Désolé ! J'ai déjà donné à un pauv' gars du Tunnel sous la Manche."

JAK, Evening Standard, 10 January 1990

"Oh look! They're going to do another estimate!"
"Tiens, regarde un peu ! V'là des gus qui viennent faire un nouveau devis !"

Immediate reactions to Eurotunnel's announcement on 13 August 1990 that 93 banks had declined to commit to the additional £2 billion loan finance sought by the Company. Opposite right: *The Economist* depicted lugubrious bankers reluctant to throw a lifeline to an anxious Alastair Morton, Eurotunnel's Chief Executive, marooned at the foot of the tunnel.

Réactions immédiates à l'annonce faite par Eurotunnel le 13 août 1990 révélant que 93 banques avaient refusé de participer au prêt supplémentaire de 20 milliards de francs recherchés par la société. Ci-contre à droite : le magazine *The Economist* dépeint des banquiers au visage lugubre réticents à l'idée de venir au secours du pauvre Alastair Morton, Directeur Général d'Eurotunnel, coincé au fond du Tunnel.

Kipper Williams, Daily Telegraph, 14 August 1990

"Votre courrier, monsieur — 93 lettres de banquiers en colère."

Keith Waite, The Times, 14 August 1990

"Just the usual message — Help! Eurotunnel."

"C'est toujours le même message —
Au secours ! Eurotunnel !"

Riddell, The Economist, 25 August 1990

In mid-September 1990 Eurotunnel was still £700 million short. Kipper Williams mimics the 'X metres to go' campaign Eurotunnel was then running to advertise the forthcoming breakthrough of the service tunnel.

A la mi-septembre 1990, il manquait toujours 7 milliards de francs à Eurotunnel. Kipper Williams exploite à sa façon la campagne publicitaire qu'Eurotunnel menait alors pour annoncer la jonction imminente du tunnel de service — "La jonction dans X mètres".

Kipper Williams, Daily Telegraph, 19 September 1990

EUROTUNNEL
Plus que 7 milliards de francs à trouver !

Smith's cartoon of an anguished Eurotunnel shareholder appeared during the rights issue in late 1990.

Le dessin de Smith, illustrant les angoisses d'un actionnaire d'Eurotunnel, fut publié au moment de l'émission de droits de souscription, fin 1990.

Smith, Independent, 1990

"Please hurry up, I've another five Eurotunnel shareholders to see before lunch."

"Voyons, dépêchez-vous ! J'ai encore cinq actionnaires d'Eurotunnel à voir avant le déjeuner !"

87

NATIONAL PERCEPTIONS
SENSIBILITES NATIONALES

Cartoonists have enjoyed a field day using the tunnel to illuminate the countless differences in national styles and character between the English and French. Of these two nations at the ends of the tunnel, it is the English who seem to have suffered more from the prospect of its construction. A centuries-old sense of being an inviolate island, a traditional aloofness from continental conflicts in favour of a widespread empire, a marked resentment of change and particularly of technological progress — all combined to generate substantial initial antipathy to the idea of the tunnel. For the French, in their fashion equally fervent nationalists, these issues have scarcely arisen and the tunnel is largely regarded as a useful piece of infrastructure. The irony is that, if all the forecasts are fulfilled, Britain will, at least in the early years, provide a substantial proportion of the tunnel's business. Despite their general suspicion of 'abroad', the British have now become enthusiastic travellers, and many have developed a special passion for France. By contrast, the French, blessed with a more favourable climate, prefer on the whole to holiday within France, and Britain remains very much a minority taste.

"In the event of war, pull!"

Dickinson, Financial Times, 8 January 1986

"Do you get the feeling that the British would really prefer a fixed link under the Atlantic?"

"N'avez-vous pas l'impression que ces British préféreraient une liaison permanente sous l'Atlantique ?"

Les caricaturistes n'ont pas manqué de se servir du Tunnel pour mettre en lumière les innombrables divergences qui séparent les Anglais des Français, de par leur style et leur tempérament. Des deux nations à chaque extrémité du Tunnel, ce sont bien les Anglais qui semblent avoir le plus souffert à l'idée de sa construction. La conviction, forgée par des siècles d'histoire, d'appartenir à une île inviolable, la froideur de toujours face aux conflits du continent pour se préoccuper davantage d'un vaste empire, une hostilité marquée à l'égard du changement et notamment vis-à-vis de tout progrès technologique, sont autant de facteurs qui ont provoqué, au premier abord, une aversion notable à l'égard du Tunnel. Pour les Français, qui, à leur manière, sont animés d'un nationalisme tout aussi farouche, ce genre de question n'a pratiquement jamais été soulevé et la majorité se borne à considérer le Tunnel comme une infrastructure utile. Or, à en croire les prévisions, l'ironie veut que ce soit la Grande-Bretagne qui s'apprête à assurer une proportion considérable du trafic transmanche, du moins pendant les premières années. Malgré leur méfiance innée à l'égard de l'"étranger", les Britanniques sont devenus des globe-trotters enthousiastes, et nombre d'entre eux entretiennent une prédilection toute particulière pour la France. En revanche, les Français, qui bénéficient d'un climat plus favorable, préfèrent dans l'ensemble passer leurs vacances en France et la Grande-Bretagne n'attire certainement qu'une minorité d'entre eux.

The characters of two dominant leaders have helped to shape the mutual perceptions of the British and French in recent years. General de Gaulle (President of France 1958-69) remained a profound nationalist and was highly sceptical of Britain's commitment to Europe; in 1963 and again in 1967 he vetoed Britain's application to join the European Community. Though an enthusiastic friend of the tunnel as a private-sector project, Margaret Thatcher (British Prime Minister 1979-90) often conveyed the impression that Europeans were not her favourite people and never relinquished her hostility to European political and financial union, the issue that finally brought about her resignation. In 1964, the French and British governments announced their joint approval of a proposal to build a Channel Tunnel. Here General de Gaulle comments ironically on the future British link with the Continent.

Au fil des dernières années, c'est la personnalité de deux figures politiques dominantes qui a contribué à forger l'image que se font les Britanniques des Français et réciproquement. Le Général de Gaulle (Président de la France de 1958 à 1969) demeura toute sa vie animé d'un profond nationalisme et se montra toujours sceptique à l'égard de l'engagement de la Grande-Bretagne vis-à-vis de l'Europe. A deux reprises, en 1963 et en 1967, il mit son veto à l'entrée de la Grande-Bretagne dans le Marché commun. Quant à Margaret Thatcher (Premier Ministre de la Grande-Bretagne de 1979 à 1990), bien qu'elle soit un supporter enthousiaste du Tunnel sous la Manche en tant qu'initiative du secteur privé, elle fit souvent sentir que les Européens étaient loin d'être ses "chouchous" et elle ne cessa de se montrer hostile à tout rapprochement permettant de consolider l'union politique et financière européenne, attitude qui allait finalement la contraindre à démissionner. En 1964, les gouvernements français et britannique annoncent leur décision commune d'approuver une proposition de construction d'un Tunnel sous la Manche. Ici, le Général de Gaulle ironise sur "l'à-peu-près" de cette nouvelle union.

Jacques Faizant, Le Figaro, 1964

**The English finally sign up for the tunnel.
Work begins in 1964.**

"Well, well! They'll almost be friends, almost European, almost continental on their little almost-island!"

Cummings, Daily Express, 22 January 1986

"We're on strike until you bring the Archbishop of Canterbury to exorcise the ghost of de Gaulle!"
"Nous ferons grève jusqu'à ce que l'Archevêque de Canterbury nous débarrasse du fantôme de De Gaulle."

Cummings conjures up the ghost of de Gaulle two days after President Mitterrand and Prime Minister Thatcher announced at Lille that their governments had agreed to the construction of the Channel Tunnel.

Cummings invoque le fantôme du Général de Gaulle deux jours après l'annonce faite à Lille par le Président Mitterrand et le Premier Ministre britannique, Mme Thatcher, de la décision commune de leurs gouvernements de construire le Tunnel sous la Manche.

93

Mrs Thatcher resigned on 22 November 1990, less than two weeks before the breakthrough of the service tunnel, in which she and President Mitterrand had been invited to participate. Right, her husband Denis, a keen golfer, finds the silver lining in her resignation. In Faizant's cartoon, opposite, she reassures him that they will earn a living by begging (= faire la manche) under the tunnel, while a puzzled tunnel worker enquires whether Maggie is ill.

Mme Thatcher démissionna le 22 novembre 1990, moins de deux semaines avant la jonction du tunnel de service, événement auquel elle était invitée à participer, au côté de François Mitterrand. A droite, son mari Denis, féru de golf, voit le bon côté de sa démission. Dans le dessin de Faizant, ci-contre, elle rassure son mari en lui expliquant que pour gagner leur vie, ils iront faire "la manche" sous le Tunnel, tandis que sur un autre, un employé du Tunnel s'inquiète de ne pas la voir à l'occasion des célébrations.

Langdon

"If Maggie does resign, it'll save her having to shake hands in the Chunnel with Mitterrand."

"Si Maggie démissionne, ça lui évitera d'avoir à serrer la pince de Mitterrand dans le Tunnel !"

Jacques Faizant, Le Figaro, 24 novembre 1990

"And what are we going to live on now?"

"Don't worry, Dennis! There's always the tunnel...
We'll scrape through!"

Seiler, Var Matin Republique, 7 décembre 1990

"I can't see Maggie anywhere... Do you think she's ill?"

Rioting football fans, rock music versus accordion tunes, illicit Parisian liaisons, frogs, beret-sporting onion-sellers — these potent national stereotypes all provided subject-matter for cartoonists.

Supporters de football belliqueux, musique pop ou accordéon, aventures parisiennes, grenouilles, vendeurs d'oignons coiffés d'un béret — ce sont là des stéréotypes nationaux évocateurs qui ont amené de l'eau au moulin des humoristes.

Cummings, Daily Express, 13 August 1986

AVIS ! NOTICE !
Tunnel sous la Manche remplacé par Mur de l'Atlantique pour tenir à l'écart les hooligans anglais

"No need to rescue them! They're British football fans cast away by the captain of a ferry."
"Pas la peine de leur porter secours ! Ce sont des supporters anglais abandonnés par le capitaine d'un ferry…"

Steve Way, Punch, 17 February 1989

"Ces Français, ils n'ont jamais su faire de la musique pop !"
"Les ouvriers refusent de continuer : ils ne captent plus que la radio française !"

Soon after breakthrough, a rumour (strongly denied by Eurotunnel) circulated that, after the first borehole was driven between the French and British sections of the service tunnel, French tunnellers dispatched a frog to their English counterparts.

Peu après la jonction du tunnel de service, la rumeur (vivement réfutée par Eurotunnel) prétend qu'une fois le premier trou de forage reliant les deux parties du tunnel de service terminé, les ouvriers français envoyèrent une grenouille à leurs homologues anglais.

Ged, The Times, 13 March 1991

"Veuillez-vous abstenir de commentaires racistes, je vous prie."

No racist comments, please

GED

Giles, Daily Express, 21 January 1986

"It'll be much more fun knowing your wife could hop over in three hours."
"Ce sera bien plus drôle quand on saura qu'en trois heures, ta femme risque de débarquer !"

ALB, International Freighting Weekly, 27 May 1991

"We're looking for personnel who have a positive attitude to the culture of their cross-Channel colleagues..."

"Nous recherchons des individus qui sachent faire preuve d'une attitude positive à l'égard de la culture de leurs collègues d'outre-Manche..."

At times during the late 1980s and early 1990s it seemed that sheep and cows formed the staple diet of Anglo-French relations. Protesting French farmers attacked lorry-loads of English lambs. These are imported live since, if killed in France, they qualify as French lamb, while carcass imports have to be marketed as English lamb, which does not sell as well. Following an outbreak of BSE (bovine spongiform encephalopathy) or 'mad cow disease' in England, many continental countries including France banned the import of English cattle. In 1991 Eurotunnel announced that it would not carry live animals for slaughter through the tunnel.

A plusieurs reprises depuis la fin des années 1980, la viande d'agneau et la viande de boeuf semblent avoir été au menu des relations anglo-françaises. Les paysans français en colère s'en prirent à certains camions transportant des moutons anglais. Ceux-ci sont importés vivants, puisque s'ils sont abattus en France, ils tombent sous l'appellation "agneau français", tandis que les importations de carcasses doivent être commercialisées sous le terme d'"agneau anglais", ce qui porte préjudice aux ventes. A la suite d'une épizootie d'encéphalopathie bovine spongiforme, dite maladie des "vaches folles", en Angleterre, un grand nombre de pays européens, y compris la France, décrétèrent un embargo sur l'importation de bétail anglais. En 1991, Eurotunnel annonça que le transport d'animaux destinés à l'abattage ne serait pas assuré par le Tunnel.

Johnston, Eveninmg Standard, 3 December 1990

"Don't be silly, Jacques, there won't be any sheep through for ages!"

"Ne sois pas si bête, Jacques. Il faudra attendre des lunes avant de voir arriver un mouton."

"When it's finished there'll be herds of mad English cows streaming through."

"Une fois le tunnel terminé, 'y aura des troupeaux entiers de vaches folles anglaises qui vont déferler."

Matt, Daily Telegraph, 1 June 1990

Bill Caldwell, Daily Express

"**Fill it in quick!**"
"**Vite ! Rebouchez !**"

Allo Allo was the title of a popular comedy series on British television based on the exploits of the French wartime Resistance. When the tunnel workers selected by ballot to undertake the breakthrough met under the Channel, the Frenchman, Philippe Cozette, managed a few words of English, while Graham Fagg, his English counterpart, knew no French at all.

Allo Allo était le titre d'un feuilleton populaire comique diffusé sur les écrans britanniques qui ironisait sur les exploits de la Résistance française. Lorsque les deux techniciens, tirés au sort pour effectuer le percement final, firent la jonction sous la Manche, le Français, Philippe Cozette, parvint à prononcer quelques mots d'anglais, mais Graham Fagg, son homologue anglais, ne connaissait pas un mot de français.

Millington, New Civil Engineer, 5 October 1989

"Euh... 'Allo 'Allo !"

Andrew, 1987

"Allo Allo !"

Second thoughts. One important reason for British opposition to the tunnel was the feeling that it would deprive Britain of her island status and so destroy a critical facet of her national identity.

Arrières pensées. Un argument de poids pour les détracteurs britanniques du Tunnel sous la Manche était le sentiment que la construction d'une liaison permanente ferait perdre à la Grande-Bretagne son caractère insulaire, détruisant ainsi une caractéristique primordiale de son identité nationale.

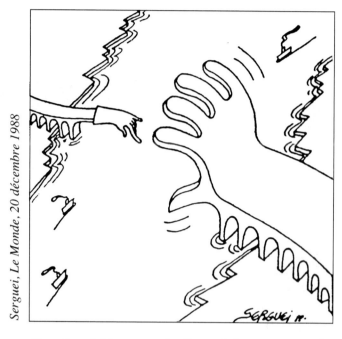

Serguei, Le Monde, 20 décembre 1988

Plans for a bridge across the Øresund, the narrow stretch of water that divides Sweden and Denmark, have met considerable opposition. This cartoon, drawn to illustrate Swedish hesitation, could equally apply, in French eyes, to British attitudes to the tunnel.

Les plans relatifs à la construction d'un pont traversant l'Øresund, l'étroit bras de mer qui sépare la Suède du Danemark, ont soulevé une forte opposition. Pour les Français, ce dessin, publié pour illustrer la valse-hésitation suédoise, pourrait tout aussi bien s'appliquer aux attitudes britanniques à l'égard du Tunnel.

"Oh come on sir, the French aren't that bad!"
"Allons Monsieur, soyez raisonnable ! Les Français ne sont pas de si mauvais bougres !"

SENSIBILITES NATIONALES

Mac, Daily Mail, 1 November 1990

"Sacrebleu! It is wet concrete! Zey have bunged up their side again!"

"Nom d'un pétard ! Le ciment est encore frais ! Ils ont une fois de plus tenté de reboucher leur côté !"

Tom Johnston, Sun

"Sacrebleu! I think it's Madam Thatcher!"
"Nom d'une pipe ! J'crois bien qu'c'est Madame Thatcher !"

When the tunnel opens, French and British police —
'flics' and 'bobbies' — will co-operate even more closely
on security and other matters. To prevent cross-Channel
misunderstandings, a group of linguists from the
University of Cambridge was commissioned to devise an
international 'policespeak' to be adopted by both forces.

Lorsque le Tunnel sera mis en service, les polices
française et britannique — les "flics" et les "bobbies" —
devront collaborer encore plus étroitement en matière de
sécurité et autres. Afin d'éviter tout risque de
malentendus, un groupe de linguistes de l'Université de
Cambridge s'est vu confier la délicate mission d'élaborer
un lexique international, baptisé "policespeak", des mots
et expressions à adopter par chacune des forces.

Le Monde, 12 septembre 1990

Field, New Civil Engineer, 20 November 1986

Opposite bottom: some alternative uses for the tunnel!

Différentes perspectives du Tunnel sous la Manche !

RAIL LINKS

LIAISONS FERROVIAIRES

The story of the high-speed rail links between the tunnel and the two capital cities represents a case-study in contrasting national attitudes. In France, where the economic benefits of the tunnel and the importance of investment in the national infrastructure have never been seriously disputed, the proposal for a high-speed line, the TGV nord, between Paris and Brussels, with a spur to the tunnel mouth at Calais, was accepted quickly and without fuss. Indeed, the only noteworthy dissent came from the city of Amiens, which found itself by-passed when the route through Lille was selected. What a contrast with the opposite side of the Channel! Proposals for a dedicated high-speed rail route through Kent to London remain firmly stuck on the drawing-board, and its completion date slips further into the twenty-first century. Until then, the new international trains will run on existing track, admittedly improved, which is also used by conventional services.To the despair of the vast majority of observers, who argue for shifting as much traffic as possible by rail rather than road and who believe that Britain's economy will be held back by the failure to up-date her rail infrastructure, very little progress has been made. Three or four years of doubt and uncertainty ended in October 1991 when the British government announced a route to King's Cross via Stratford in east London. However, many doubts remain about its financing and timetable, accompanied as the announcement was by statements indicating that the new link is not required before the year 2005. France moves forward to implement a strategic high-speed rail plan while Britain remains a branch line.

Trog, Observer

Sélection de King's Cross comme second terminal du Tunnel

"Ces pauvres grenouilles, ça n'leur dirait sans doute rien de se retrouver à Waterloo !"

La question des liaisons ferroviaires à grande vitesse entre le Tunnel et les deux capitales constitue à elle seule une étude de cas très parlante sur les différences entre les comportements nationaux. En France, où personne n'a jamais véritablement contesté les avantages économiques du Tunnel et l'importance que revêt l'investissement au niveau des infrastructures nationales, la suggestion d'une ligne à grande vitesse, le TGV Nord, entre Paris et Bruxelles, qui prévoit un embranchement jusqu'à l'entrée du Tunnel au niveau de Calais, fut approuvée rapidement et sans faire d'histoires. De fait, le seul mécontentement qui mérite d'être mentionné fut celui de la ville d'Amiens, qui se trouva à l'écart du réseau à l'issue de la sélection du tracé passant par Lille. Quelle différence avec l'attitude rencontrée de l'autre côté de la Manche ! Toute proposition en faveur d'une ligne à grande vitesse spécialisée qui traverserait le Kent pour regagner Londres n'a jamais dépassé le stade de projet et la date de mise en service ne cesse d'être reportée, s'enfonçant toujours un peu plus dans le XXIe siècle. En attendant, les nouveaux trains internationaux devront circuler sur la voie actuelle, rénovée, certes, mais qui reste la ligne empruntée par les services conventionnels. Au désespoir de la grande majorité des observateurs, qui souhaiteraient voir les chemins de fer, et non le réseau routier, assurer le plus possible de trafic et qui estiment que l'économie de la Grande-Bretagne sera freinée par la vétusté de ses infrastructures ferroviaires, bien peu de progrès a été accompli. Finalement, le gouvernement britannique mit un terme à trois ou quatre années de doute et d'incertitude lorsqu'en octobre 1991, il annonça que l'itinéraire retenu rejoindrait King's Cross en passant par Stratford, à l'est de Londres. Pourtant, bien des doutes subsistent aujourd'hui quant au calendrier et au financement du projet ; en effet, l'annonce était accompagnée de déclarations précisant qu'une telle liaison ne serait pas requise avant l'an 2005. Tandis que la France va de l'avant dans la mise en oeuvre de son plan stratégique de liaison ferroviaire à grande vitesse, la Grande-Bretagne en reste au stade d'une ligne secondaire...

Ward, Railnews, January 1986

"He's determined to be first through the tunnel."
"Qu'est-ce que tu veux... Il s'est mis dans la tête d'être le premier à traverser le Tunnel..."

Danziger, Christian Science Monitor, 5 November 1990

**Projet de terminal du Tunnel sous la Manche,
côté britannique**

Two cartoons reflecting the widespread astonishment at Britain's failure to build a high-speed rail link between London and the Kent coast in time for the opening of the tunnel.

Deux dessins qui traduisent l'étonnement général devant l'inaptitude de la Grande-Bretagne à construire une liaison ferroviaire à grande vitesse entre Londres et la côte sud, qui soit en service au moment de l'ouverture du Tunnel sous la Manche.

LIAISONS FERROVIAIRES

"Will passengers from the French high-speed train arriving from Paris transfer to the number 11 tram for King's Cross!"

"Les passagers du TGV en provenance de Paris sont priés de monter dans le tramway No. 11 à destination de Londres. Merci."

Banx

"I'm an English high-speed train."

"Permettez-moi de me présenter.
Je suis un TGV anglais."

Left: A French TGV locomotive meets its English counterpart, modelled on the engines that appear in the celebrated Thomas the Tank Engine railway stories for children by the Rev. W. Awdry. The English, romantics when it comes to steam traction, proved less enthusiastic when confronted with the prospect of a high-speed line through their neighbourhood.

Opposite: JAK's TGV crawls through the Kent countryside in a scene reminiscent of the early days of motoring, when vehicles had to be preceded by a pedestrian carrying a red warning flag. Hollingbourne was one of the villages that feared the high-speed link would threaten its rural tranquillity.

A gauche : un TGV français rencontre son homologue anglais, qui ressemble fort à la locomotive héroïne de Thomas the Tank Engine, célèbres histoires pour enfants écrites par le Rév. W. Awdry. Les Anglais, nombreux à garder la nostalgie des trains à vapeur, se sont montrés beaucoup plus réticents à l'idée d'un TGV qui traverserait leur paysage.

Ci-contre : le TGV de JAK se traîne dans la campagne du Kent sur une toile de fond évocatrice des débuts de l'automobile, lorsque les engins devaient suivre un piéton qui annonçait leur passage en arborant un drapeau rouge. Hollingbourne est l'un des villages qui craignaient de voir leur vie paisible menacée par une liaison à grande vitesse.

JAK, Mail on Sunday, 17 June 1989

LIAISONS FERROVIAIRES

"Look Dad, it's one of those fast French trains."
"Oh regarde, Daddy, c'est un de ces trains rapides français !"

JAK, Mail on Sunday, 29 January 1989

"Don't worry about the view sir, you won't be able to see the high-speed trains for the Toyota car plant."
"Monsieur, ne vous inquiétez pas pour la vue ! Des TGV, vous n'en verrez point ; l'usine Toyota masquera tout ça !"

Many retired people were active in the protest groups that sprang up to oppose the various routes through rural Kent that British Rail proposed for its high-speed line. At the same time, attempts were being made to attract commercial and industrial investment to the less prosperous eastern part of the county.

Un grand nombre de retraités se rallièrent aux divers groupes de protestation qui se constituèrent çà-et-là dans le comté du Kent pour s'opposer aux différents itinéraires avancés par British Rail pour sa ligne à grande vitesse. Parallèlement, on assista à maintes tentatives pour amener des sociétés industrielles et commerciales à investir leurs capitaux dans les régions moins prospères de l'est du comté.

**SNCF — the next TGV for London has been delayed
due to: leaves on the line**

Austin, New Scientist, 14 July 1988

Travellers waiting for a London-bound TGV find it delayed because of 'leaves on the line'. Each autumn, trains on British Rail's Southern Region are cancelled or delayed for this reason; the leaves cause the traction wheels to slip or prevent current being picked up from the third rail.

Des voyageurs se voient contraints de patienter pour prendre le TGV à destination de Londres, retardé en raison de "feuilles sur la ligne". Chaque automne, les trains du Réseau Sud de British Rail sont annulés ou retardés pour ce motif. Les feuilles font patiner les roues des trains ou empêchent le passage du courant électrique par le troisième rail.

Mahood, Daily Mail, 13 December 1990

**"Probably the logo for the new high-speed
Channel Tunnel link."**

**"C'est sans doute le logo de la nouvelle liaison à
grande vitesse pour le Tunnel sous la Manche."**

The high cost of building a dedicated high-speed line across Kent and through densely populated South London suburbia was a major factor in its frequent postponement. Mahood's symbol for the new line merges British Rail's own logo with £ signs.

Le coût de construction élevé d'une ligne spécialisée à grande vitesse qui traverserait le Kent et les banlieues densément peuplées du sud de Londres constituait un argument dissuasif permettant de justifier son perpétuel ajournement. Ici, Mahood transforme adroitement le logo existant de British Rail en un motif qui n'est pas sans rappeler le symbole de la livre sterling.

Prada, L'Idiot international, 2 août 1989

"It's mine, it's mine, it's mine!..."

"Euh... I'm the Amiens shuttle service"
(150,000 inhabitants and 30 miles away).

In contrast with the residents of Kent, the citizens of Amiens fought hard for the high-speed line to be routed through their city, rather than via Lille. Prada's cartoon, opposite, shows the two cities squabbling like small children, while PIEM mourns the line's absence.

Aux antipodes des résidents du Kent, les habitants d'Amiens se sont farouchement battus pour que la ligne à grande vitesse traverse leur ville au lieu de passer par Lille. Le dessin de Prada, ci-contre, se gausse des deux villes qui se chamaillent comme des gamins, tandis que PIEM compatit aux malheurs de la ville.

"When the weather's fine, you can even see the TGV."

J.B. Roussel, Courrier Picard, 3 octobre 1989

At one point in its campaign, the Amiens-Picardie TGV Association bought a 15-hectare plot of land on the proposed route through Lille, split it into thousands of portions and sold them to supporters, thus forcing SNCF to embark on lengthy compulsory purchase negotiations.

L'un des stratagèmes auxquels eut recours l'Association TGV Amiens-Picardie durant sa campagne fut d'acquérir une parcelle de terrain de 15 hectares que devait traverser l'itinéraire lillois. Elle s'empressa de la diviser en des milliers de parcelles et de vendre chaque lot à ses supporters, forçant ainsi la SNCF à s'embarquer dans de pénibles négociations d'expropriation.

Rail link frustrations. Right: in an adaptation of *The Angelus* (1855-57), Jean-François Millet's depiction of rural piety, two peasants rest from their labours as they hear the TGV passing through Amiens.
Below: immediate reactions to the British government's announcement in October 1991 that, while the high-speed link between London and the tunnel would indeed be built, it was not scheduled to open until the year 2005.

Frustrations pour un chemin de fer... A droite : dans une adaptation du tableau de Jean-François Millet, *L'Angélus* (1855-57), qui dépeint la piété du monde rural, deux paysans interrompent leurs travaux lorsqu'ils entendent le TGV traverser Amiens.
Ci-dessous : réactions immédiates à l'annonce faite par le gouvernement britannique en octobre 1991 qui, certes, confirmait la construction d'une liaison ferroviaire à grande vitesse entre Londres et le Tunnel sous la Manche, mais précisait qu'elle ne serait pas opérationnelle avant l'an 2005.

"I think I can hear the TGV passing through Amiens."
"Be quiet and pray!"

Calman, The Times, 8 October 1991

"Nous regrettons de vous annoncer que le prochain train à destination de PARIS aura quatre mois de retard..."

Paul Thomas, Evening Standard, 8 October 1991

"My daughter calls him Eurotunnel."

"Ma fille l'appelle Eurotunnel."

123

ALB, International Freighting Weekly, 8 July 1991

"Will you stop singing 'And the Train Ran Right Thro' The Middle Of The House'... you'll get us lynched!"
"Arrête donc de chanter "Le p'tit train traverse la campagne"... tu vas nous faire lyncher !!"

Throughout 1991 the merits of two rival routes for the long-anticipated rail link across Kent and into central London provoked considerable controversy and emotion, especially in Kent itself. The eventual, somewhat unexpected, choice of the northern route to King's Cross via Stratford compelled British Rail to abandon several years' work planning the southern route it had favoured. The decision removed blight from one set of homes and families only to impose it on another.

Tout au long de 1991, les mérites respectifs des deux itinéraires rivaux proposés pour la liaison ferroviaire tant attendue, traversant le Kent pour arriver au centre de Londres, furent à l'origine de bien des controverses et bien des débats passionnés, notamment dans le Kent. En fin de compte, lorsque, contre toute attente, c'est la route passant plus au nord, pour rejoindre King's Cross via Stratford, qui fut retenue, British Rail se vit obligée d'abandonner plusieurs années de travaux de planification sur la route sud, pour laquelle elle avait un penchant. Cette décision ne fit que soulager un groupe de foyers pour en accabler un autre.

"The Channel Tunnel Link isn't coming through here after all dear!"
"Chéri, en fin de compte la liaison du Tunnel sous la Manche ne passera pas par ici !"

Brookes, The Times, 16 October 1991

Brookes, The Times, 11 October 1991

Widespread controversy was aroused by the decision of the British government, announced at the annual conference of the Conservative Party held at Blackpool in October 1991, to postpone the completion of the rail link until the early years of the twenty-first century. Left: Prime Minister John Major, caricatured as a steam locomotive from one of the Rev. Awdry's children's stories, slams into the buffers. Below: on Blackpool beach, John Major confronts a sea of electoral troubles.

La décision du gouvernement britannique, rendue publique lors de la conférence annuelle du parti conservateur organisée à Blackpool en octobre 1991, de retarder la réalisation de la liaison ferroviaire jusqu'au début du XXIe siècle, ne manqua pas de faire couler beaucoup d'encre.
Ci-dessus : le Premier Ministre britannique, John Major, représenté sous la forme caricaturale d'une locomotive à vapeur, héroïne des histoires pour enfants du Rév. Awdry, entre en collision avec les butoirs. A gauche : sur la plage de Blackpool, John Major doit faire face à une vague de troubles électoraux.

Economie — Services sociaux — Europe — Liaison Tunnel sous la Manche

Brookes, The Times, 14 October 1991

BANK *of* ENGLAND
BILLIONS OF *POUNDS*

EUROTUNNEL

George Stephenson 1781–1848

Banque d'Angleterre — milliards de livres

In October 1991, Eurotunnel announced a further increase in the forecast cost of the project and also became embroiled in renewed financial disagreements with its contractor, Transmanche-Link. Here George Stephenson, railway engineer and designer of *Rocket*, the world's first passenger railway locomotive, sheds a tear at the increasing cost of the tunnel. Stephenson's portrait appears on the back of the new, smaller-size £5 note issued by the Bank of England in June 1990.

En octobre 1991, Eurotunnel annonça une nouvelle augmentation des coûts prévisionnels. Elle se trouva également plongée dans un nouvel imbroglio financier avec son entrepreneur, Transmanche-Link. George Stephenson, ingénieur des chemins de fer et constructeur de *Rocket*, la première locomotive à vapeur au monde pour train de voyageurs, essuie une larme devant la flambée des coûts du Tunnel. Les nouveaux billets de cinq livres, plus petits que le modèle précédent, émis par la Banque d'Angleterre en juin 1990, sont à l'effigie de Stephenson.

ACKNOWLEDGEMENTS
REMERCIEMENTS

Eurotunnel would like to thank all those connected with the Channel Tunnel project, staff members and other friends alike, who have helped with the research, writing and production of this book. Particular thanks are due to the translators, Maryck Nicolas and Trevor Holloway in association with First Edition Translations, Cambridge, and to Geoffrey Beare, author of *The Illustrations of W. Heath Robinson: a Commentary and Bibliography* (Shepheard-Walwyn, 1983), for his assistance with the pages dealing with Heath Robinson's cartoons.

The illustrations in the book have been provided by the following sources and copyright holders. While every effort has been made to supply information concerning original sources and to secure permission to reproduce, we may have been unable in a few cases to discover the relevant information or to trace the copyright holder.

No illustration may be reproduced without the express permission of the copyright holders.

Eurotunnel tient à remercier toutes les personnes liées au projet du Tunnel sous la Manche, membres du personnel ou autres amis, qui ont contribué à la compilation, la rédaction et la réalisation de cet ouvrage. Nous tenons notamment à remercier les traducteurs, Maryck Nicolas et Trevor Holloway, en association avec First Edition Translations, Cambridge, ainsi que Geoffrey Beare, l'auteur de *The Illustrations of W. Heath Robinson: a Commentary and Bibliography* (Shepheard-Walwyn, 1983), pour l'aide qu'il nous a apportée au niveau des pages traitant des dessins de Heath Robinson.

Les illustrations contenues dans cet ouvrage ont été obtenues auprès des sources et des titulaires de copyright mentionnés ci-après. Si nous avons tout mis en oeuvre pour dûment citer les sources de ce matériel et pour obtenir les autorisations nécessaires à sa reproduction, il se peut, dans quelques cas très rares, que nous n'ayons pas été en mesure de découvrir les informations nécessaires ou d'identifier le titulaire du copyright.

Aucune illustration publiée dans ce livre ne saurait être reproduite sans l'autorisation expresse des titulaires du copyright.

Andrew front cover, 65, 103; David Austin 35, 83 (top), 119 (left); Hector Breeze 62 (top); © C Charillon, Paris 72, 92, 95 (left); Christian Science Monitor © 1990 TCSPS 114; the Daily Mail 63, 83, 106, 117, 118, 119 (right); © the Daily Telegraph Ltd 76; © the Daily Telegraph Ltd, 1973 52; © the Daily Telegraph Ltd, 1987 18; © the Daily Telegraph Ltd, 1989 69 (top); © the Daily Telegraph Ltd, 1990 84, 86; Evening Standard 9, 68 (top and bottom), 83 (bottom), 105, 115, 123 (bottom right); by permission of Express Newspapers 17, 93, 96, 98 (bottom), 101; reproduced by permission of the executors of the late Geoffrey Dickinson of the Financial Times 78 (top), 79, 90 (right); Wally Fawkes/The Observer 112; Walter Goetz 23, 29; Mrs Miriam Hardy 113; Hulton Picture Company Ltd 40; the Indpendent 56, 78 (bottom), 87; Tom Johnston 100, 107; Gray Joliffe 16; Chantal Meyer-Plantureux 62 (bottom); New Civil Engineer 58-59, 60-61, 64, 102, 108 (bottom), 109; Denis Pesin 77 (top); Private Eye 53; reproduced with permission of Punch 15, 24-25, 30-31, 34, 37, 39, 42, 43, 44, 45 (left and right), 46, 47, 57, 66 (left), 71 (right), 91, 97; Rex Features/News International 125; Chris Riddell 82 (bottom), 85 (right); the Estate of Mrs J. C. Robinson 48, 49 (left and right); 50 (left and right), 51 (left and right); Bart Roozendaal 65 (top); Jean-Bernard Roussel 122; Albert Saunders 69 (bottom), 80, 99, 124; David Simonds 73; Spectator 77 (bottom); © Times Newspapers Ltd, 1966 21; © Times Newspapers, 1991 98 (top), 123 (bottom left), 126 (top and bottom), 127; Keith Waite 82 (top), 85 (left); Whitbread plc 67.